A MORAL TALE

Children's Fiction and American Culture,

1820-1860

James relieving the wants of little Robert. (See p. 36.)

A
Moral Tale

Children's Fiction and American Culture

1820 -1860

by Anne Scott MacLeod

ARCHON BOOKS / 1975

Library of Congess Cataloging in Publication Data

MacLeod, Anne.
   A moral tale.

   Bibliography: p.
   Includes index.
   1. Children's stories, American—History and criticism.
2. United States—Social conditions—To 1865. I. Title:
Children's fiction and American culture, 1820-1860.
PN1009.A1M24   813'.3'09   75-12533
ISBN 0-208-01552-3

© 1975 by Anne Scott MacLeod
First published 1975 as an Archon Book,
an imprint of The Shoe String Press, Inc.,
Hamden, Connecticut 06514

Printed in the United States of America

To my mother and to the memory of my father.

Contents

Acknowledgements

Like any author, I have acquired debts along the way to publication. The greatest of these I owe to Dr. David Grimsted, who read and reread the manuscript at every stage and whose criticisms and encouragement—both— were invaluable to me. Dr. Donald Gordon, Dr. Otho Beall, Dr. Miles Bradbury and Dr. James Flack also contributed helpful suggestions. Mrs. Ann Shore, who typed the manuscript, is a perfectionist in her work and I am most appreciative of the care she expended so unstintingly on my words. To my own family, for their interest and moral support, I am always grateful.

Introduction

Middle-class Western society, of which American society is perhaps the purest example, has made the family the central institution of its private life. And the middle-class family has increasingly made children—their welfare, their education and their happiness—the focus of attention in the home.[1] In the United States of the early nineteenth century, rapidly changing social conditions accelerated and intensified the process that made children the objects of so much adult interest, hope, and anxiety. Nationalism and optimism, reforming zeal and a concern for the perpetuity of democratic institutions, all contributed to the extraordinary attention Americans turned upon their children. Convinced that young Americans were the inheritors of prospects unique in human history, Americans examined every aspect of childhood and child nurture in an effort to ensure that the rising generation would be equal to the challenge and the promise of the future.

While hopeful expectation underlay much of this early nineteenth-century concern with children, there were less clearly acknowledged feelings involved as well. Interest was sharpened by anxiety in a society changing so rapidly; emphasis on the right direction of children reflected doubt as much as hope, fear as often as optimism. American reponse to change was ambivalent, and American concern for the next generation encompassed both sides of that response.

The same interaction of social and intellectual forces which produced such interest in children also stimulated the creation of a new literature for them. The rise of an American fictional literature written expressly for children and designed to cater —however reservedly—to their taste for amusement was almost entirely a nineteenth-century phenomenon. Though books for children had existed in America since the earliest settlements, they were, nearly without exception until the latter eighteenth century, instructional literature of one kind or another.[2] Even after the Revolution, when acceptance of fictional literature for children grew, the American production of such books was negligible; most nonschool juvenile books were imported or pirated from Europe and England.

During the first half of the nineteenth century, however, and especially after 1820, American preoccupation with the future of the republic and with the children who would shape that future was reflected in a greatly increased production in the United States of all forms of literature for children, including fiction. By 1860 there were hundreds of nonschool books available in the United States which had been written by American authors for American children. The books were literarily very limited—narrow, stilted, and wholly given over to didacticism. No child today reads even one of these pre-Civil War fictional storybooks. Except as a stage in the development of children's literature, they are largely forgotten.[3]

Yet the literature written for children in any period provides an interesting, if sometimes oblique, source for the study of cultural history. Children's stories are almost invariably prescriptive, to a greater or lesser degree; they present the approved values of society to children.[4] At the same time, juvenile literature is one vehicle by which a society conveys to its young a picture of the world outside childhood. But since few adults, and perhaps fewer authors of books for young people, are entirely frank or wholly realistic in what they tell children about the world, any view of reality in children's literature is refracted through adult attitudes toward children and society, with the result that juvenile stories are often a suggestive for what they leave out as for what they include. Death and poverty, for instance, were a commonplace in the children's literature of antebellum America —but no child character was seen to defy authority successfully. By contrast, the young heroes of later books, from *Tom Sawyer* to *Peter Rabbit* and beyond, flout adult restriction and survive— but there has been little mention in the twentieth century, until very recently, of death and social hardship.

In the case of frankly didactic juvenile fiction, like that

written between 1820 and 1860, communication of many social and individual values was direct; authors conceived and constructed the literature to indicate to children how they expected them to behave, what they wanted them to value, where they wished to see them seek happiness or fulfillment. Early American children's stories, designed for the express purpose of teaching morality to the younger generation, clearly stated many of the accepted truths of their time. Less directly and less consciously, in descriptions of reality and in admonitions to the young, the literature also revealed the kind of apprehensions the authors felt about life in their era. Since adults tend to project upon children both their hopes and their fears about the future, the value of children's fiction as a source of social history exists on both the conscious and the unconscious levels. It is useful for what it has to say directly about the values the authors hoped to teach children, and it is equally interesting for what it suggests about the fears, the anxieties, and the doubts of its creators.

As an index to the realities of an historical era, of course, fiction at any level has certain limitations. The view it provides is often personal, sometimes mythic or deliberately distorted; rarely is it an effort to see a period whole, or even factually. But if literature is not documented history, (and is not meant to be), if it is only a partial view of a past time, it is a valuable one for all that. "History and literature are records of internal and external experience. Both attempt to gain from experience some kind of insight into the quality, mood, tempo, and personality of life—not just the *fact* of the past, but the *feel* of it."[5] Literature offers an avenue of understanding leading into the imaginative and emotional experience of people in time; it reverberates with those beliefs and assumptions which go into the cultural outlook of a particular society in a particular era. Some of the more elusive aspects of the American past have been illuminated through examination of literature in such studies as William Taylor's *Cavalier and Yankee*, R. W. B. Lewis's *The American Adam*, and Henry Nash Smith's *Virgin Land*, to name but a very few.

From the point of view of the historical researcher, popular literature, created for and read by a mass audience, has as much value and often fewer limitations for cultural understanding than literary productions more distinguished as art. Popular literature deals in the common, if unexamined, canons of belief widely accepted in a given time and place; it is less likely than serious literature to be a strongly personal or idiosyncratic statement by the author. It can, and often does, provide an index to those ideas which have become a part of the day-to-day life of a society and a guide to that working synthesis of the ideal and the real which is at the base of the broad cultural outlook of any period. Often better than works of singular genius, popular writing suggests to the cultural historian the conventions and the commonplaces of an era. And better, too, than the complexities and the subtleties of serious literature, the simplistic plots and characterizations of popular fiction may reveal the common expectations and the widespread anxieties of a society.[6]

Popular literature has attracted some students of social history. Helen Papashivly's *All the Happy Endings* explored some of the motives and emotions behind nineteenth-century domestic novels; Constance Rourke used popular writings in her survey of American humor; John Cawelti examined that recurrent American idol, the self-made man, as he appeared in popular novels as well as in success manuals and guides. The tremendous success of Horatio Alger's subliterary creations of the post-Civil War period has drawn the attention of several cultural historians who wanted to understand why Alger spoke so successfully to that generation of Americans. Their analyses, in turn, have cast light on the myths and realities of a complex period in American history.[7]

Children's fiction written before 1860 shared many of the advantages of popular literature as a repository of broadly accepted social and moral attitudes. Such writing was a new endeavor for Americans, undertaken entirely for didactic purposes, and it attracted few authors of genius or even of outstanding talent.[8] There was little creative imagination or highly personal vision in these stories; stylistically and ideologically they were remarkably similar to one another. Like other forms of popular literature, they mirrored the conventional thought of the dominant middle class in their time; indeed, their didactic reason for being ensured that they would promulgate accepted ideas almost exculsively and blur or obliterate controversy. The very lack of imaginative freedom that blighted them as literature gives them solidity as an historical resource.

This literature has rarely been examined for what it can reveal about the cultural tone or the social concerns of its time. Monica Kiefer studied American children's books of the eighteenth and early nineteenth centuries in order to assemble a picture of American child life during that period. More recently, Bernard Wishey's interesting work, *The Child and the Republic*, used children's fiction as one of many sources through which he traced changing approaches to child nurture in the United States between 1830 and 1900. In *Guardians of Tradition*, Ruth Elson examined nineteenth century American attitudes as they were expressed in the school books of the time. And, of course, there are a number of works which treat nineteenth-century American children's fiction in the context of the general history of children's literature.[9]

Some of these studies use juvenile fiction as an indication of the child's world. Certainly there is value in this perspective since some relationship always exists between how children view the world and how their stories predispose them to view it. Yet, because the literature was written by adults out of adult ideas of the risks and requirements of the world beyond the home, it reflected primarily adult social opinion. And because a fictional literature required that ideas be incorporated into a framework of story, even the most didactic narratives conveyed, better than unadorned advice or exhortation, something of the emotional context of the social attitudes put forward in the tales. In the codes and conventions of this juvenile fiction lie deep echoes of the "quality, mood, tempo and personality" of American society between 1820 and 1860.

The material used in this study is original fiction written for children by American authors in the period between 1820 and

1860. It does not include school books, poetry, manuals of advice, or translations and rewritings of classic or folk literature. I have also excluded those basically informational "stories" which hung pages of fact upon a very slender framework of narrative. These consisted mostly of imagined conversations between adult and child in which the child asked leading questions and the adult answered with paragraphs of informative discussion. Though the line between didactic fiction and pedagogy with a patina of fiction is sometimes hazy, it can usually be drawn in a rough way.

The study is confined to the fiction meant for children, as nearly as that can be determined. The definition of childhood was none too precise in the period, but it seems to have ended usually at about twelve years old.[10] Beyond that age, children were presumed to be interested in such adult topics as marriage, employment, and servant problems; there was "no adolescence" in antebellum America, as Tocqueville observed.[11] Some literature, ambiguously addressed to "young persons," was clearly meant for those who had passed beyond what the authors called childhood; other books so dedicated were just as clearly meant for children. Decisions in such cases were made on the basis of content.

The literature was chosen to be representative of the children's fiction produced in the period. I have made no attempt to select what was best from a literary standpoint; and, indeed, the good was so very exceptional in this period, and the rest so very much greater in bulk, that it is the rest that must furnish material for generalization. I have, however, compared the least known with the best known of the authors, and have found the differences negligible from the point of view of social history.

Assessments of the popularity of these books are difficult. Few publishers' records survive, and those that have are generally conceded to be unreliable.[12] Reminiscences and autobiographies seem to indicate that Jacob Abbott's and Samuel Goodrich's books were among those best remembered by adults, but both of these authors wrote so many more books

14

than any of their contemporaries that it is hard to be sure what this means. In any case, the strong similarities among all these stories in theme, style, and approach make the question of popularity of particular tales less important than it would be for a more varied literature. In the juvenile fiction written before 1860, the prototype overshadows any idiosyncrasies of particular authors and stories.

Questions about whether American children read these books, and about what they thought of them if they did read them, cannot be answered conclusively. Autobiographical accounts like Lucy Larcom's, William T. Venable's, and Edward Everett Hale's offer some evidence for the most reasonable supposition: that early nineteenth-century children both read and enjoyed, selectively, the fiction written for them. Lucy Larcom found a story by Lydia Maria Child "the joy of my heart to read, though it preached a searching sermon to me." Edward Everett Hale was "seduced up into the attic" when a new number of *The Juvenile Miscellany* was there. William Taylor Venable read Mrs. Sigourney's "Pictorial Reader" when he was about eight years old, though "with some disdain for its wish-washiness."[13] Certainly print was the mass media most available for entertainment, and reading was the commonest form of purchasable amusement in the nineteenth century.

The relentless moralizing of this literature oppresses most twentieth-century adults who read it, and some have assumed that nineteenth-century children must have been equally oppressed by it.[14] But such judgments are both unhistorical and out of keeping with what we know of children and their moral attitudes—unhistorical because the morality in children's books was not more omnipresent nor more insistent than that in most fiction, drama, and poetry for adults; a fervent concern with morality was simply part of the nineteenth-century outlook, and presumably nineteenth-century people found the emphasis unobjectionable. And children, particularly, are not put off by strong and simplistic morality in their literature; on the contrary, that is how they themselves tend to view the world. As Jean Piaget has said, "moral obligation forms part

15

of the very structure of the child's mind."[15] It is precisely the clarity of perfectly identifiable evil predictably defeated by an equally knowable good that has kept folk and fairy tales in the realm of children's literature when they have passed out of the category of adult entertainment. Only when moral preaching gets in the way of the story do children reject it—and then it is the preaching, not the morality, to which they object.

The focus of this study, however, is not on the children who were the subjects and objects of the literature, nor on the reality of their lives. Taken by itself, the children's fiction of any era would be a doubtful source of information about how children actually live and think, and certainly the juvenile fiction of 1820 to 1860, morally purposeful but bare-bones thin as literature, offered no more than an occasional glimpse of the daily lives of real children. What the literature furnished in abundance was an insight into what adults wanted for and from the children of that time, and what their desires for children revealed about their own attitudes.

An example will suggest what answers I think can and cannot be properly derived from this literature. The whole press of the fiction was toward early solidification of an autonomous personality in children. In conjunction with the anxious view of the outer world presented in the books, such an approach suggested that the authors saw early self-definition as a form of protection against the hazards of living. Richard Sennett has theorized that the desire for early and fixed self-definition is a defense against the chaos of disordered, confusing experience of the real world: "This fixed self-definition gives [those who adopt it] a strong weapon against the outside world. They prevent a pliant traffic between themselves and men around them and so acquire a certain immunity to the pain of conflicting and tangled events that might otherwise confuse and perhaps even overwhelm them."[16]

This speculation, I think, corresponds with some—though not all—the motives behind the urgent moral didactism of children's fiction before 1860. But the anxiety revealed in the books was that of the adults who wrote them, not of the children who read them. Whether the children of the period tried to counter the fluidity of their society by early fixing the boundaries of their characters cannot be established from this literature. That the authors wanted to induce them to do so is unquestionable.

The period that produced the literature considered in this study was a time of great turbulence for American society. The unrest and uncertainty of American life gave impetus to that intense emotional investment in home and hearth which was so characteristic of the age. When Americans developed a fictional literature for their children in the years between 1820 and 1860, it was an expression of their concern with home and children, certainly. They hoped to preserve and support the function of the home in their changing society, and they hoped to pass intact to children the mores in which they strongly believed. But their motives were also bound up in their judgments about the contemporary state of their society and about its future, even about its survival. The fiction they produced speaks of all these concerns and more. It was clumsy literature, conceptually impoverished and insistently preachy, but it radiated sincerity, on the whole, and kindliness, and a strong sense of personal moral responsiblity. Where these qualities proved inadequate to the challenges of the time, the literature also registered, obliquely but unmistakably, the uneasiness of antebellum American society.

I

"*Let Their Minds Be Formed, Their Hearts Prepared*"

This is a day of peculiar care for Youth. Christians feel that their children must be trained up for Christ. Patriots and philanthropists are making rapid improvements in every branch of education. Literature, science, liberty, and religion are extending in the earth. The human mind is becoming emancipated from the bondage of ignorance and superstition. Our children are born to higher destinies than their fathers; they will be actors in a far advanced period of the church and the world. Let their be minds be formed, their hearts prepared, and their characters moulded for the scenes and duties of a brighter day.[1]

From these opening words in his 1827 prospectus for a new magazine, Nathaniel Willis, founder of *Youth's Companion*, went on to outline how he intended to aid in the important work of preparing American children for the scenes and duties which awaited them. He proposed to establish

a small weekly journal, which should entertain . . . children and insensibly instruct them; which should occupy leisure hours, and turn them to good account; which should sanction and aid parental counsel and pulpit admonition; which should, in an easy and familiar manner, warn against the ways of transgression, error and ruin, and allure to those of virtue and piety.[2]

The prospectus expressed sentiments very widespread in the America of its period. It *was* a time of "peculiar care for Youth," and it was as well a time of great faith in the power of the written word to form the mind, prepare the heart and mold the character of a growing child. Indeed, the editor of *Youth's Companion* encompassed in this passage most of the assumptions which underlay the development of an American fictional literature for children before the Civil War. Of these, the most important by far was the conviction that the future of an American child was unique and uniquely promising, and that his prospects—that "brighter day" to which he was born—demanded a literature shaped to his special circumstances.

"It is for the books of early instruction, in a great degree, to lay the foundation on which the whole superstructure of individual and national greatness must be erected," wrote one early author of American juvenile fiction. He regretted that "the greater part of the juvenile books in the United States are foreign," for such books, however worthy, "give a wrong direction to the minds of the young, modelled as they are on a condition of life, and on prevailing sentiments, civil, moral and social . . . varying from those which American children should early be taught to cherish."[3] Many Americans after 1820 agreed. They were suddenly dissatisfied with the imported books that had been the general literary fare available to their children till now; they wanted American books for their children of destiny.

So moved by national feeling, a remarkable number of Americans took up their pens, as did the author of *Jack Halyard*, expressly to provide "American books for American children."[4] They wrote to fill a national void, like Lydia Maria Child, whose preface to *Evenings in New England* justified her attempt to follow such illustrious English authors for children as Mrs. Barbauld and Maria Edgeworth by pointing out that their works were "emphatically English," while she herself could offer "American scenes and American characters."[5] Many authors of children's books wrote anonymously; many more were such minor figures that it is difficult to document their lives except in the sketchiest ways. Their motivation, however, is well substantiated, and their products were remarkably alike in conviction, construction and character. Hundreds of very similar little books "insensibly instructing" American youths were written between 1820 and 1860. The production of juvenile literature by American authors, which was only a trickle in the 1820s, had become a steady stream by the 1830s and a positive torrent by the 1850s.

In this shift from foreign to native authorship, children's books were part of a general trend in book publishing in the United States. Few reliable figures are available, but Samuel Goodrich's estimates have been widely accepted as guides.[6] According to Goodrich, thirty percent of the books published in America in 1820 were of American authorship and seventy percent British. His figures show that by 1850 the balance had been reversed.[7] Goodrich pointed out that much of this increase in American authorship was due to the enormous production of schoolbooks by American authors. While separate figures for children's fictional books do not exist, it seems likely—based on the evidence of publisher's lists, catalogues, and special collections—that juvenile fiction followed a pattern similar to that of the whole publishing field. To this impressionistic evidence, Goodrich also contributed contemporary testimony. Writing in 1856, from the viewpoint of one whose concern with the production of children's books had been his bread and butter for more than three decades, he said:

> In casting my mind backward over the last thirty years—and comparing the past with the present, duly noting the amazing advances made in every thing which belongs to the comfort, the intelligence, the luxury of society—there is no point in which these are more striking than in the books for children and youth. Let any one who wishes to comprehend this matter, go to . . . a juvenile bookstore . . . and behold the teeming shelves—comprising almost every topic within the range of human knowledge, treated in an attraction of style and every art of embellishment—and let him remember that nineteen twentieths of these works have come into existence within the last thirty years.[8]

One sizable contribution to both the bulk and the concept of juvenile fiction arose out of the Sunday School movement, mostly from the publishing activities of the American Sunday School

Union. The ASSU, uniting the Sunday School efforts of the major evangelical Protestant sects, was founded in 1824 as part of the great evangelical movement of the early nineteenth century, and grew with remarkable rapidity. Within eighteen months there were 400 branches of the organization in twenty-two of the twenty-four states and territories. The Union became, in a very short time, a publisher of formidable productivity. By 1830 it had issued some six million copies of Sunday School works and was spending $76,000 annually. These figures reflect more than children's books, of course; the ASSU published literature for all ages: periodicals, tracts, and even song lyrics that provided clean replacements for the old ribald verses to popular tunes. But books for children, and particularly books of fiction, were probably the most influential product of the Union. "Sunday stories," as they were called, were distributed to Sunday School libraries, which were not only free, but often the only circulating libraries in a community. They reached many a child who had few other sources of reading material.[9]

The Union's determination to reach a broad audience directed its choices concerning the forms of literature it produced for children. All literary forms were put in the service of moral evangelism, including history, biography, poetry, and—most surprising—fiction. The decision to publish fiction for children was not taken lightly; it was reached only after brisk debate within the organization.[10] For fiction, in the early nineteenth century, was of dubious repute. Often considered frivolous at best and depraved at worst, fiction was thought a dangerous influence on children. "Books of light reading," warned one author, "are as numerous and injurious as the plagues of Egypt. . . . The ruin of many a young man may be traced to the influence of bad books."[11]

But nineteenth-century Americans also recognized the attraction stories held for children, and the Union was prepared to be pragmatic. If children would read stories more readily than tracts, then the Union would furnish stories, though, of course, only those written in "strict accordance with truth and nature."[12] And the ASSU did publish stories, by the hundreds, until its demise in 1860.

Fictional literature published by the ASSU was not narrowly religious; in fact, there is little useful distinction to be made between most Sunday stories and those produced for children by secular publishing companies. ASSU books were carefully nonsectarian. Every book issued by the Union was reviewed by a board of laymen representing the major evangelical sects. No work was published which did not have the unanimous approval of all the board members. When necessary, books were revised by the board to remove controversial sectarian elements. As a result, the children's stories lacked all traces of the inner conflicts of early nineteenth-century Protestantism; the edges of sectarian disputes were deliberately blurred and indistinct, and the message conveyed by most Sunday School stories was more broadly moral than specifically religious. While ASSU books had some special features, notably their frequent endorsement of Sunday School attendance and an acceptance of the doctrine of natural depravity until well into the 1850s, they were, on the whole, nearly indistinguishable from most secular juveniles. The shared religious assumptions and moral standards of the two bodies of writing far outweighed the differences between them.

Certainly the fact that the ASSU regarded fiction not as a form of entertainment for children but as an instrument for their moral instruction in no way divided Sunday School publications from secular tales. Almost all fiction in the first half of the nineteenth century, whether for children or for adults, was justified by its didactic properties: even so dedicated an entertainer as Anthony Trollope believed that the object of a novel should be to instruct in morals. Authors of children's stories were particularly careful to underline the instructive qualities of their works. "I am well aware that conscientious scruples are entertained by many wise and good people as to the use of fiction in juvenile books," wrote Samuel Goodrich in the preface to a book of stories, "but it appears to me that the argument commonly lies against the *abuse* and not against the *use* of fiction."[13]

By abuse of fiction, Goodrich meant the telling of imaginative tales, especially fairy tales, which he, with most of his generation, deplored. These tales he thought "calculated to familiarize the mind with things shocking and monstrous; to cultivate a taste for tales of bloodshed and violence; to teach the young to use coarse language, and cherish vulgar ideas. . . . Had it been said that these books were calculated to make criminals of a large part of the children who read them, I think the truth would have been . . . fairly stated."[14] In the same vein, Cardell remarked with some complacency in the preface to *The Happy Family* that his book "owes nothing to Blue Beard, or any other giant, nor from a wisard or wisard's pen, nor magic lamp; nor fiddling cats, nor motherly talking goats." On the contrary, "the design was to make the narrative true to nature, to correct principles, and the conditions of ordinary life."[15]

Fiction was to deal with reality and to instruct, and it was instruction that came first. As Goodrich explained very frankly to his young readers in a foreword addressed to them, "When I tell you stories of things that never happened, my real design is to give you lessons of importance. . . . I have mixed with these stories some good and useful things."[16] Even much later, in 1857, that relatively flippant author, "Fanny Fern", echoed the sentiment, though her remarks showed that the balance between the goals of entertainment and instruction had begun to shift. Of her *Play-Day Book* she said, "I made it to read when you are out of school, and want to be amused. If, while you are looking only for amusement, you should happen to find instruction, so much the better."[17]

The chief target of fictional instruction was the moral character of the young; every work of fiction written for children before 1860 was dedicated to the moral education of its readers. Fiction attempted "to excite attention to good things by entertaining matter; and yet everything frivolous or injurious [was] avoided."[18] Some also bristled with useful information about the world; many "stories" were little more than fictional dialogues between adult and child in which the adult imparted knowledge—on the physical properties of water, the products of Brazil, the botanical features of North America—to an obligingly attentive

child. But whether or not they were larded with factual infor-
nation the stories were invariably concerned with moral edifi-
cation. The first aim of fiction for children was "to present models
of good conduct for imitation and bad examples to be shunned, to
explain and enforce the highest principles of moral duty."[19]

In a literature meant to prepare American children for
their happy future, such concern with principle and moral character, such dedication to "good and useful things," was central. A
democratic society, as Jefferson had early pointed out, ultimately
depends upon the virtue and intelligence of the people. This view
was part of the conventional wisdom of the time. Catherine
Beecher, in her *Treatise on Domestic Economy*, treated it as
truism:

> The success of democratic institutions, as is conceded by all,
> depends upon the intellectual and moral character of the
> mass of the people. If they are intelligent and virtuous,
> democracy is a blessing, but if they are ignorant and wicked,
> it is only a curse.[20]

Catherine Maria Sedgwick reiterated these sentiments and indicated their implications for the moral training of the young:

> That the safety of the republic depends on the virtue of the
> people is a truth that cannot be too assiduously taught;
> and that it is the business of the young, as well as of the old,
> to help on the cause of goodness, cannot be too strongly
> impressed.[21]

There was a special urgency behind all this concern for the
virtue of the people. By the 1820s, the United States was thoroughly committed to a course of widening political and social democracy; the national movement in that direction was not often
seriously or openly opposed. Nearly all Americans, the writers
of children's books among them, not only accepted the inevitability
of an increasingly democratized society, but also hailed it as one
of the glories of the nation's future.

At the same time, it was evident to all who took a responsible interest in the future of the country that democratic society was particularly vulnerable to the consequences of ignorance, lawlessness, and immorality on the part of its citizens. The specter of the French Revolution, with its total breakdown of social order, still haunted the consciousness of the "settled classes," and Shays' Rebellion, though it was more than thirty years in the past, was for many still a vivid reminder that social disorder was not an exclusively European phenomenon. Increasingly after 1820, the development of large urban centers with growing areas of poverty and the mounting numbers of immigrants, often poor and uneducated, made "old world" problems seem ominously intrusive in the United States.

It seemed clear, then, to the thoughtful and the anxious that if democratic freedom was to be extended to nearly everyone, then the safety of all was dependent upon the right influences being brought to bear, and early, upon every American child. Education was an indispensable protection for the Republic: in *The Duty of American Women to Their Children* (1845), Catherine Beecher warned that if the United States continued to ignore its two million unschooled children, the nation might suffer bloodshed and anarchy. She spoke, as she so often did, for many of her contemporaries. The second quarter of the nineteenth century fairly rang with the cry for "rational education" of the young and for the closest attention to the molding of "pliant minds." The social, public function of such education was usually explicit: "The positive influence of early and judicious instruction is the only safe dependence for public virtue."[22]

But this was no plea for intellectual training. Nineteenth-century Americans were persuaded that the salient influences on society were moral rather than intellectual, and that a democracy was far more dependent upon the right *feelings* of its citizens than upon their cultivated knowledge. Not formal schooling alone, but the whole development and training of children became the focus of much serious attention. Indeed, in the opinion of many Americans, formal schooling was the least of the matter. Far more important than "mere" factual knowledge was the molding of character. It was character that made the man and

26

ensured the democracy; it was moral training that shaped character. "The glory and efficacy of our institutions will soon rest
with those who are growing up to succeed us," wrote William
Cardell, ". . . their proper education is a subject of as high interest as any to which the human mind has ever been called. They
are the pivot of the moral world." The whole purpose of learning
in the United States must be "not to settle nice disputes in Greek"
but to "distil the love of goodness on the opening buds of intellect.[23] The content of juvenile fiction was dictated by such considerations:

> In a narrative for the general reading of children, the proper
> subjects of interest are fidelity to nature; to moral truth;
> regard to the public good; the endearing scenes of domes-
> tic life; generosity and gratitude; filial, parental and frater-
> nal love.[24]

It was always entirely clear in children's stories that intellectual
and moral qualities were not of equivalent value. One fictional
mother observed to her children that "it is far better that [one]
should know how to be kind and gentle to those around him than
to understand all the poetry, or all the science that was ever
written."[25] Another told her son, "beautiful and useful as knowledge is, that goodness and mercy opens heaven to us," and the
book's subtitle, "Goodness Better Than Knowledge," telegraphed
the moral of the whole story.[26] Nearly every author agreed with
Lydia Sigourney's observation that "education is not for knowledge or intellectual cultivation alone. It must also strengthen
the moral principle, and regulate the affections."[27] Although a
decent respect was paid to intellectual attainment, its primacy
was *always* disclaimed, and the stories themselves invariably re-
volved around moral achievements, never intellectual prowess.

In these sentiments, as in many others, children's books were
of a piece with their time. It would be difficult to overstate the
importance of the concept of morality in American society between 1820 and 1860. Rhetorical it certainly was in many cases,
and a sorry distance often stretched between the rhetoric and the

reality of a getting and grasping society; nevertheless, the ideal of Christian morality suffused nearly all popular literature of the period and all discussion of social and political issues within their covers.

The preoccupation with morality so characteristic of the era was surely in some measure a counterweight for the considerable uneasiness Americans felt about the shifting rules and values of their growing society. These forty years were a time of ever-accelerating change for Americans—social and economic, political and personal; wherever they looked, Americans saw their world in a state of flux. Many of the changes seemed promising, some were threatening, all were unsettling to some degree. In such a time, the kind of moral certainty promulgated in children's and other popular literature became more attractive as it became more elusive in reality.

For the Christian morality to which America paid so much lip service in this period was clearly at odds with much of the social and most of the economic behavior of the society. The material success so prized by Americans—most foreign visitors commented at length on the American worship of the dollar—was plainly the reward of activities very different from the ideal behavior of a Christian. The drive for economic success encouraged ambition, aggression, and a competitive apirit. Above all, it seemed to call for a concern for self and a disregard of others that was the very antithesis of the selfless ideal held out to Christians. The tension between these two goals, and the problems created for American children by the disparity between them, has been suggested by Bernard Wishey in his examination of nineteenth-century theories of child nurture, *The Child and the Republic*. It is significant that Wishey found no rational attempt by child nurture experts to reconcile the implicit conflicts between Christian upbringing and the competitive realities of the American nineteenth century.

The fact is that, on the whole, Americans found it easier to separate intellectually two such contradictory sets of values than to reconcile them. This feat was most conveniently accomplished by splitting the responsibility for moral education away from the sphere of practical matters and assigning it to those institutions already outside the political and economic arena—that is, to the home and, in a lesser degree, to religion. Religion and home, but especially home, were to keep America pure and see that her children were rightly guided, while the rest of society went about its business of growing, competing, and succeeding. Americans also assured children—and themselves—that it was home-taught morality, not aggressiveness, that guaranteed success. The theory insisted that a moral man need not seek success; he need only live and work in accord with the principles he learned at home, and success would find him out.

The burden on the home was therefore very great. Home and family bore the major responsibility for the moral training of children and thus, by implication, for the moral health of the nation. In a society constantly jostled by change, the family was the most stable social institution in view, and the only one that seemed to offer any guarantee for social stability in the future. Americans had a heavy emotional investment in the concept of the family as chief architect of private (and therefore public) morality, which goes far to explain the soaring prose in which they celebrated its sanctity: "The family seems to me a divine institution," wrote Samuel Goodrich typically. "It is . . . the anchor of society, the fountain of love and hope and dignity in man and human society."[28]

But however much tribute they might pay to the importance of home, American men were unlikely to make it the central task of their own lives. Work in the large competitive world preempted their attention; it was woman who was to rule as the heart of the home. Everyone agreed that home's burden was mostly woman's burden; the awesome duty to mold the moral character of the rising generation was hers. "It is . . . conceded," Catherine Beecher observed, "that the formation of the moral and intellectual character of the young is committed mainly to the female hand."[29]

It was more than conceded. It was hailed as a triumph of nature and a working out of God's plan for the Universe. The female hand that shaped the character of a generation was of course a mother's hand: Daniel Webster called mothers "the effective teachers of the human race."[30] The exaltation of maternal influence and of the spiritual and moral responsibilities of motherhood was a major theme through the period, and the lyricism with which it was expressed increased steadily over the course of four decades. The image of the ideal mother could be quite dazzling:

> With eyes uplifted to a protecting Heaven, she must walk a narrow path of right,—a precipice on either hand,—never submitting, in her lowliness of soul, to the encroachments of the selfish, and eager, and clamorous crown—never bowing her own native nobility to the dictation of those whom the world styles great. . . . Her children revere her as the earthly type of perfect love. They learn, even more from her example than her precept, that they are to live not to themselves, but to their fellow-creatures, and to God in them.[31]

The exaggerated rhetoric of a Maria McIntosh—which could be matched by dozens of similar effusions on the subject of motherhood—gave a clue to the emotional intensity behind the assignment of woman's role. All that was being lost in a hustling, competitive era was to be preserved in the home. All that was honored but in the breach in the practical world was to be literally performed in the ideal world of mother and child. The selflessness, the generosity, the patience and mildness that would surely pave the way to failure in a competitive society was to pave the way to heart's ease and heaven in the special domain of home. A poem, written by Sarah Hale and published in *Godey's Ladies Book*, of which she was editor, said it all:

> The outward world, for rugged toil designed,
> Where evil from true good the crown was riven,
> Has been to Man's dominion ever given;
> But Woman's empire, holier, more refined,
> Moulds, moves and sways the fallen but God-
>   breathed mind,
> Lifting the earth crushed heart to hope
>   and Heaven.[32]

From all these roots sprang the new growth of an American literature written especially for children. Nationalist fervor asked for American authorship, concern for the training of young Americans in the obligations of citizenship called for education. And the general agreement among Americans that the most important qualities of a good citizen were moral rather than intellectual tended to put the creation of books for children into the hands of those designated as the keepers of the moral conscience of American society. Since women and churchmen had been assigned the major responsibility for the moral training of the young, the writing of children's books, bent as they were to moral didacticism exclusively, was taken up largely by women and clergymen. Authorship lists are long and not always very informative, since so many of the authors wrote anonymously or under pseudonyms, but there is little doubt that, on the whole, as Catherine Beecher said, the female hand was uppermost. Women found ready acceptance in the field of writing for children, and there were a great many, needy or enterprising or both, who turned their talents to it in these years. A number of successful women authors—Eliza Follen, Sarah J. Hale, Sara Parton, and Louisa Tuthill, to name only four—embarked on their careers in writing for the most practical of reasons: they were widowed, they had children to support, and few alternatives were available to them in the working world.[33]

Some of the nation's most popular adult authors turned occasionally to juvenile fiction. Catherine Maria Sedgwick, of the prominent Massachusetts family, wrote a number of very popular and highly regarded novels. Her first efforts, *A New England Tale*, published in 1822, and *Redwood* (1824), are often considered the beginning of the American domestic novel. She also produced a few, highly didactic little fictional works aimed at "young people," of which *Love Token for Children* (1839) was probably best known.

Lydia Sigourney, "Sweet Singer of Hartford," was another very popular author of adult works who sometimes turned her hand to children's stories. Mrs. Sigourney was best known to her own generation as a poetess and author of innumerable sentimental effusions in both prose and verse. She was a prolific writer and widely published; 67 books and more than 2,000 articles, published in nearly 300 periodicals, made her name well known in her own time. Though most of her work was written for adults, much of it showed a strong preoccupation with the moral training of children and she wrote several nonfictional books of advice to young women. Like so many of the women authors of her time, Mrs. Sigourney pursued her writing career for practical as well as creative reasons. She was not widowed until late in life, but she did find it necessary to help the family fortunes after her husband's business failed.

While it was relatively easy for a writer to get his work published in the antebellum period, few authors were well paid, or could afford to be specialists. They therefore wrote whatever they could—prose and poetry, books and periodical articles, fiction and nonfiction—and they were frequently editors as well as writers. Only Samuel Goodrich was a publisher of any note, but Sara J. Hale was highly successful as the editor of *Godey's Ladies Book*; Lydia Maria Child edited the popular, though short-lived *Juvenile Miscellany*; Eliza Follen was for several years the editor of the Sunday School publication, *The Child's Friend*; and Caroline Gilman was founder and editor for seven years of *The Rosebud Magazine* for children.

Those authors whose names and backgrounds can be discovered seem to have had a good deal in common. They were middle class, Protestant, often of "old stock" American heredity. Nearly all were born in New England or the Middle Atlantic states, and lived their lives there. A southern author of children's books was an exception; a southern imprint on a child's book of fiction before 1860 was a rarity.[34] In fact, the general description Whitney Cross assigns to reformers of the same period will stand for most of the known writers of children's fiction: Yankee derivation, superior education, and at least average prosperity characterized most of them.[35]

Jacob Abbott, one of the most prolific authors of his time, was all of these. Born in Maine in 1803 and educated at Bowdoin College, Abbott was, like many of these writers, a teacher and a clergyman before he was a writer. He founded and ran the very successful Mt. Vernon School for Girls in Boston until his literary success allowed him to return to Maine and concentrate on a writing career. He was well traveled and certainly prosperous beyond the average. Only the degree of his remarkable success and the size of his literary output (more than 180 titles) set him apart from many of his colleagues in the field of juvenile writing.

For the women writers, it is hard to claim superior education in any formal sense but, for their time, most were at least well-read. Many came from well-educated families, so that their exposure to learning was relatively great, even if their own schooling was sketchy and "female" in emphasis. Catherine Maria Sedgwick and Eliza Lee Cabot Follen, both of educated, prominent New England families, were considered highly educated women in their time. Lydia Maria Child studied with her brother, Convers (who later became a professor of religion at Harvard), as long as he was at home, and maintained a lifelong intellectual comradeship with him.

To a very large degree, the authors also had in common their attitudes toward children, child nurture, and moral values. A number of them—including Abbott, Mrs. Child, Lydia Sigourney, and Louisa Tuthill—wrote books on child nurture and home management. While there were undoubtedly theoretical or theological points of difference among them, in those matters of practical morality with which children's stories were concerned they were generally agreed. Their values were traditional in most respects, yet they endorsed, broadly speaking, advanced concepts of child nurture and moral education. Like many middle-class Americans, they were ambivalent toward the changes taking place around them—embracing some, resisting others, concerned about where all the movement of the time was taking them. As a group, however, they were far more of their time than out of it. Most of them must be considered quite successful members of their vigorous society who, by writing fiction for children, were taking advantage of an opportunity to earn their livings in a new field of endeavor.

Lydia Maria Child, whose writing career lasted from 1824 to 1878, was a representative author of children's fiction in a number of respects. Born Lydia Maria Francis in 1802 in Medford, Massachusetts, she grew up in a family of comfortable circumstances. Her schooling followed the pattern for girls of her time and place; she was educated in local public schools, sent to a private seminary for one more year, then left to her own efforts for the remainder of her intellectual development. In Mrs. Child's case, a strong intellectual curiosity ensured that her education did not end with her formal schooling; it would be accurate to describe her as well educated, if not systematically or academically trained.

Like most of those who wrote for children in this period, Mrs. Child did not limit her work to children's literature, but wrote widely in the field of popular literature. Her output included popular novels, periodical articles of various kinds, books of domestic advice, and (less typically) abolitionist literature. Also like many other writers of the era, she was editor of various periodicals at various times during her career. *The Juvenile Miscellany*, which she established in 1826, was one of the earliest periodicals for children, and certainly the most successful up to that time.

She began to write because she recognized, as so many Americans of her time did, that there was a demand for American writing. Her first published work, a novel entitled *Hobomok*, was an improbable romance—but of thoroughly American surroundings—involving, among other things, a marriage between an English girl and an Indian warrior. It was published in 1824, signed only by "An American." In that same year, Mrs. Child (then Maria Francis) also wrote her first work for children, *Evenings in New England*. (It, too, appeared anonymously, but later juvenile books by Mrs. Child listed it among her works.) It was in the preface of this early book that Mrs. Child pointed to the need for American stories for American children as her reason for entering a field already occupied by such popular English writers as Maria Edgeworth and Anna Barbauld.

In writing for children, Mrs. Child was also moved by that earnest concern for the character of American children that she shared with most of her contemporaries. The first issue of *The*

Juvenile Miscellany contained an "Address to the Young," in which she told her new young audience, "I seldom meet a little girl, even in the crowded streets of Boston, without thinking with anxious tenderness, concerning her education, her temper and her principles." *The Mother's Book* indicated how she looked upon children's books; "The books chosen for young people should as far as possible combine amusement with instruction, but it is very important that amusement should not become a necessary inducement."[36] Her numerous juvenile stories reflected her efforts to amuse as well as instruct, but mostly they showed her "anxious tenderness' for those principles she thought should guide the life of a child.

Her own life was a monument to principle. To a remarkable degree, Lydia Maria Child lived by the ideals set forth in the didactic juvenile fiction of her time. She consistently put moral principle above the rewards of financial success and public approval; she worked industriously, economized, and practiced charity, combined successfully her creative life with her very burdensome domestic duties, and followed the dictates of her demanding conscience wherever they led.

They soon led away from the pleasant enjoyment of her early success as a writer into the difficult territory of the abolitionist movement. Mrs. Child's reputation as a popular novelist was established promptly upon the publication of her first book, when she was only twenty-two, and was more than matched by her success as creator and editor of *The Juvenile Miscellany*. Public reception of the *Miscellany* was enthusiastic from the first, and subscriptions increased year by year from 1826, the year of its founding, until 1833. But in 1833, Mrs. Child turned her back on popularity and economic security to join, actively and conspicuously, the abolitionist crusade against slavery.

She had always opposed slavery, as even her earliest writing for children (discussed in chapter four) indicated. Her first approach was that of moral suasion and gradualism—not an unacceptable stance in the North during the relative calm of the 1820s. Early in the 1830s, however, she was won over to the concept of immediate abolition by William Lloyd Garrison: "He got hold of the strings of my conscience and pulled me into reform."[37] In 1833, a dangerous year indeed in which to join the Garrisonian abolitionists, Mrs. Child wrote and published *An Appeal in Favor of That Class of Americans Called Africans.*

The *Appeal* came at a high point of anti-abolitionist feeling in the U.S. and quickly ended Mrs. Child's acceptance as a popular writer. "Her works were brought with avidity before, but fell into sudden oblivion as soon as she had done a greater deed than writing any of them."[38] Wendell Phillips, at her funeral, described the price she paid for her decision: "Hardly ever was there a more costlier [sic] sacrifice. . . . Narrow means just changing to ease . . . fame and social position in her grasp, every door opening before her. . . . One blow, and the spreading tree is dead."[39]

She herself was not surprised; she had anticipated the hostile reaction, and her words in the preface to the *Appeal* echoed the advice offered to children in innumerable juvenile tales: "I am fully aware of the unpopularity of the task I have undertaken; but though I *expect* ridicule and censure, I do not *fear* them."[40] And to her brother, who in 1835 urged her to be more careful, she wrote, "You ask me to be prudent, and I will be so, as far as is consistent with a sense of duty; but this will not be what the world calls prudent. Firmness is the virtue most needed in times of excitement."[41]

The Juvenile Miscellany died in 1834, subscriptions having fallen off "to a ruinous extent" after the appearance of the *Appeal.*[42] Mrs. Child continued to write articles and books of popular literature for adults and for children, as well as abolitionist propaganda. She also edited *The National Anti-Slavery Standard* for eight years, from 1841 to 1849. But financial ease was lost forever; she and her husband had need the rest of their lives for all the economizing skills she had described in *The Frugal Housewife.*

Yet, there was never any indication in either her correspondence or in her published writing that Lydia Maria Child regretted her choices. Within the limits of human reality, she seemed to find that there was satisfaction, if not creature comfort, in a life lived strictly in accord with principle—as the children's books always promised. Certainly her idealism and strength of character in the face of opposition "won respect," as juvenile fiction also always prophesied, from such distinguished contemporaries as John G. Whittier, William Ellery Channing, Wendell Phillips, Charles Sumner, and many others.[43]

Samuel G. Goodrich, author of the Peter Parley books for children and surely the most prolific author of juvenile literature of his era, was as representative of his time as Lydia Maria Child, but his career in the field of children's books diverged from the usual pattern at several points. He was neither a teacher nor a clergyman, but a man of business who made the writing and publishing of children's books nearly the whole of his very profitable trade; of his 170 works, about 120 were "professedly juvenile."[44] During most of his life, he made his living entirely by the production of children's books, which no other writer of his time was able to do.[45]

Goodrich was born in Ridgefield, Connecticut, in 1793, sixth child of the Congregational minister of that town. The family was of moderate means and some prominence in Connecticut: one of Samuel's uncles was mayor of New Haven for nearly twenty years, and two others were members of Congress; his uncle, Chauncey Goodrich, was successively a congressman, a senator, and mayor of Hartford. In spite of a strong family tradition that favored extensive education—one grandfather was a Doctor of Divinity, the other a physician—Samuel Goodrich showed no great taste for learning, and finished his formal education after less than a year of high school. At the age of fifteen, he went to work as a clerk in his brother-in-law's country store. He left store clerking within a few years, but remained in business; by 1816 he was engaged in book selling and publishing in Hartford.

His achievements in the book trade were modest until 1826, when he moved his business to Boston and began to write children's books, having early observed that they offered "a large field for improvement."[46] He wrote and published the first Peter Parley book, *Peter Parley's Tales of America*, in 1827.

His success, once he had entered the juvenile field, was enormous and almost immediate. Eventually, according to his own figures, he was author or editor of some 170 volumes, of which approximately seven million had been sold by 1856, or about 300,000 annually.[47] The greater number of the books Goodrich produced were nonfiction—geographies, histories, botanies, readers, and other school books of various kinds. Most of the Peter Parley "tales" for which he was most famous were basically informational, with only the thinnest veneer of story laid over collections of facts. Even the more truly fictional stories, such as *Peter Parley's Juvenile Tales* and *Peter Parley's Fables*, were considerably stiffened with factual information, in addition to the moral exhortation—a device used, of course, by many other authors of fiction to ensure the usefulness of their efforts.

Goodrich was led to writing for children, in part, by a good businessman's instinct for a market. He recognized that Americans were extraordinarily interested in the education of their children; in an age of opportunity, he observed that "[the] desire of improvement is . . . extended to the children, and animates the bosom of every parent."[48] Another part of his motivation was supplied by strong convictions about what kind of literature was useful and improving for children to read. He was vehemently opposed to the old folk and fairy tale literature as children's fare, and had been, according to his own account, even as a child. His impression then was that "children's books were either full of nonsense, like 'hie diddle diddle' in *Mother Goose*, or full of something very like lies, and those very shocking to the mind, like *Little Red Riding Hood*." Books of fantasy and violence— "the old monstrosities"—were corrupting influences, Goodrich was sure: "Had it not been for the constant teaching of rectitude, by precept and example, in the conduct of my parents, I might, to say the least, have been seriously injured."[49] His models for suitable literature he also found as a boy in Hannah More's *Cheap Repository Tracts*. Twenty years after his joyous discovery of Mrs. More's *Entertaining, Moral and Religious Tales*, he launched his project of "making a reform—or at least an improvement—in books for youth," to bring to American children a literature as benign and improving as the *Moral Repository*.[50]

Whatever part moral idealism played in his original decision to write for children, there is no doubt that Goodrich's long career in that endeavor was sustained and shaped by practical necessity. "The needs of my family require me to continue grinding at the mill," he wrote to a friend in 1855.[51] He has often been considered a hack writer,[52] and the label is in large measure deserved. For Goodrich, the production of children's literature was a business and a livelihood, and he did not hesitate to manufacture new books out of old, rewriting the same material again and again, incorporating the writing of other authors, and hiring writers to "compend" textbooks to be produced under the magic name of Peter Parley. Such practices were by no means peculiar to Goodrich, of course; many writers of the day used similar devices to extend their production. Certainly, Lydia Sigourney, the "sweet singer of Hartford" who was as popular a writer as Goodrich, matched him in her willingness to reuse her own creations endlessly and to imitate—sometimes very closely—the styles and successes of other authors.[53] The hack work showed; though the first Peter Parley books had a certain freshness, many of the later tales were mechanical and often perfunctory, even in their moral conviction. In the end, Goodrich himself said, "I have written too much and have done nothing really well."[54]

Different as their careers were, Lydia Maria Child and Samuel Goodrich together well represent the amalgam of idealism and practicality, of nationalistic pride and anxiety for the future of the republic, of kindly interest in children and moral didacticism that went into the creation of an American literature for children. They wrote, as did all those who produced the children's fiction of the period, "openly, avowedly, to attract and please children,"[55] but this was never their whole aim, nor even the most important part of it.

Like most of their countrymen, writers of juvenile fiction were caught up in a preoccupation with the future. The American Republic, in the eyes of many of its citizens, was the last, best hope of mankind, whose fate would prove or disprove the workability of democracy as a modern form of government. Faith in the democratic experiment was strong, and authors like to dwell upon the singular opportunity which was the heritage of American children. But faith was tempered by anxious thought; the glorious American future held as much responsibility as opportunity, these writers believed, as much threat of collapse as promise of fulfillment. Democracy would stand or fall by the moral qualities of its citizens, and these in turn were dependent upon the early training of the young. No task was therefore more full of portent for the American future than the moral education of its youth. The more glowing the vision of the future a writer offered, the more heartfelt were his admonitions on the importance of moral character. Juvenile literature, conscientiously designed to "enlarge the circle of knowledge, to invigorate the understanding, to strengthen the moral nerve, to purify and exalt the imagination."[56] came into being, not to entertain children, but to prepare them for their momentous role in the preservation of the Republic.

II

"True to Nature . . . and the Conditions of Ordinary Life"

According to its creators, the fiction written for children before 1860 was realistic. Stories of fantasy, adventure and imagination could not advance and might even interfere with the moral education of the young. Indeed, fiction of any kind, even the most straightforward, since it was by definition "not true," was always under some suspicion and had constantly to be justified by its useful qualities as a teacher of morality. The only acceptable juvenile fiction was that offering clear moral lessons which children could apply directly to their daily behavior. Therefore, the children's stories were meant to be and the authors often claimed they were "true to nature . . . and the conditions of ordinary life."[1]

In fact, of course, the realism in juvenile books was always subordinated to didacticism. Both consciously and unconsciously, the authors edited reality in order to teach morality, with the result that the "real world" as it appeared in the literature was a curious mix of truth and distortion, of acceptance and denial of things as they were. It was a muted world that served as background for these moralistic narratives, vague in outline and constricted in dimension. At the same time, it was a place in which many of the harsher features of human existence—death, disease and despair—were visible as they have rarely been in children's books since. The books both reflected and distorted the society that produced them. They were not so much a mirror of their time as a composed picture of what the writers believed children needed to know about the world in order to survive in it, to impose order upon it, to take moral responsibility, and to cope with whatever life brought them by way of success or failure. They were less a factual than an emotional portrait of an era.

For the most part, the literature was narrow, domestic and

serious-minded, "portraying generally such conduct, and expressing such sentiments and feelings, as it is desirable to exhibit and express in the presence of children."[2] The boisterous, colorful, aggressive and active society that gave it birth was present largely by implication, at least until the 1850s. The authors dealt with social realities, but their handling revealed little understanding of the economic or social structure of their society and still less of how the fate of an individual might become intertwined with the larger social movements of his time. The views on display in the stories were earnest but simplistic; the complexity of human life in general and of American society of the period in particular was implicitly denied, passed over in favor of moral certainty.

The compass of nearly all children's stories in the period was markedly restricted. In spite of their professed interest in producing books especially for American children, the authors seldom drew upon the American experience for their material. They rarely told the story of pioneers or immigrants; they ignored the wilderness except as scenery, and the encounter with Indians, wild animals or other physical danger, which was to be the staple of one genre of children's reading in a later era, was absent from most children's books before the Civil War. History was a subject for school books, not for fictional tales; the authors dealt almost entirely with their own time, with only an occasional reach as far into the past as the Revolutionary War. Flights of imagination were limited to a few—very few—rather labored allegorical morality tales like C. M. Sedgwick's "The Chain of Love"[3] or Lydia Maria Child's occasional "fairy tales."

The authors of juvenile fiction imposed the constraints upon themselves in the name of duty, and for the sake of giving to children what they thought children should have, although they were often well aware that children might prefer more exciting fare. "It would be easy to make a story more fascinating, by crowding it with incitements to eager curiosity, or highwrought wonder; but its tendency would, in that case, be mischievous. It is not with such seasoning that the tender mind should be fed."[4] Tender minds were given instead innumerable small tales of temptation resisted, anger restrained, disobedience punished, and forbearance learned. Countless desirable traits of character were developed and strengthened, and undesirable ones "rooted out" in the pages of fictional books for children. High adventure was rare; high ideals were universal.

The pervasive tone was serious. There was little laughter and less humor in the stories; gaiety and lightheartedness were, at most, very restrained. All emotion, in fact, was restrained in its expression—grief as well as joy, satisfaction as much as anger. To a child who had done a kind deed, and who showed her pleasure in it, her mother remarked, "My dear child, I advise you, when you have any thing to do for any one, to think only of them, and not of yourself; and then you will be in no danger of vanity."[5] Children were expected to be thoughtful rather than spontaneous, and ideal adults were shown as rational rather than emotional in their relations with each other and with children.

A serious mood was perhaps inevitable in such a highly didactic literature; certainly, the limitations of the fiction should not be regarded as evidence that adults of the period thought of children as "miniature adults." On the contrary, the concept of childhood as a stage of life distinct from adulthood was well developed by the early nineteenth century,[6] and the growth of this literature was itself an effort to meet children at what the authors conceived to be their level. Though they may not have understood children or their tastes very well, these writers certainly looked upon them as beings unlike adults in important ways, and made some effort to take their tastes into account when they wrote for them. At the same time, because they were embarked upon a project of the most consequential nature, authors saw no place for frivolity or "mere amusement" in children's books. In writing for children, they were shaping "pliant minds" and forming the moral character of the rising generation; they had in view "the character and state of future millions, in this world and the next."[7] The fiction, therefore, addressed the future good of children above all else, underwriting the philosophy of the fictional parent who reproved her idle child so gently and so seriously: "It grieves me to distress you, my dear; but your future usefulness, happiness, and respectability, are more important than your present ease."[8] So, too, did writers of juvenile fiction put a child's future character before his present amusement.

Preoccupation with inner development undoubtedly goes far to account for the characteristic lack of atmosphere in juvenile fiction before 1860. Except for those "stories" which were really only vehicles for information, this literature gave small attention to the physical world. There was little local color or sense of place in them, for the authors had their thoughts firmly fixed on the messages they wished to deliver, and they rarely paused to make backgrounds vivid or specific. The physical surrounding of juvenile tales was neutral and hazy, quite lacking in the descriptive detail that gives conviction and definition to fictional writing.

The commonest settings were vaguely pastoral, with trees, streams and hills all described very generally: "They resided on a well-cultivated farm; a brook spread its crystal waters in front of the house, and beyond it were hills."[9] Or, "The farmhouse was situated on a sequestered road, on both sides of which the farm extended to a considerable distance, and looked in as beautiful order as any gentleman's garden."[10] Early in the period, descriptions of the countryside were almost uniformly simple and sparse. Later, especially in the 1850s, authors sometimes incorporated the conventionally "romantic" nature descriptions so dear to popular writers of the period: a "cottage home" might be located "on the brow of a woody hill" with a "clear, running brook" somewhere nearby, and a "velvet lawn" all around.[11] But the neutral quality persisted; it is seldom possible to identify places in children's tales with any certainty. Even Jacob Abbott, who was more given to literary detail than most of these authors, presented Franconia, scene of his quite lively series of tales published in the fifties, only as "a place among the mountains at the North."[12]

Cities figured much less frequently than did the country in the stories, but the paucity of description and specificity was similar in both cases. Boston could not be distinguished from New York or Philadelphia in most children's fiction, nor could large cities be easily discerned as different from those of only moderate size. There were few clues about how the buildings and streets looked, what kind of transportation people used, or where they worked. Markets, shops, newspapers, holidays, and entertainments are all missing from typical stories. The boarding houses so frequently mentioned by foreign visitors as distinctive features of American cities in the Jacksonian era did not appear in children's books.

The terms used to describe cities were either neutral ("bustling" and "crowded") or hostile ("smoky and unwholesome").[13] No juvenile author seems to have admitted to liking cities, at least not in children's stories, though several of them lived in the nation's largest cities.[14] Whenever they contrasted city life with country life, these authors invariably endorsed country living. Like Jefferson, they identified the yeoman farmer, "possessor of true independence," with morality and the safety of the republic. "Sheltered from those rushes and reverses, which in crowded cities await those who make haste to be rich, [the farmer] feels that patient industry will ensure a competent support for himself and family," wrote Lydia Sigourney. Mrs. Sigourney, who lived all her adult life in Hartford, believed that the farm was "the true order and nobility for a republic." Those virtues which might "fly from the pomp of cities . . . will be found sheltered in safety and honor, amid the farmhouses of our land."[15]

Hers was very much the accepted view. Farm life, "simple" and "wholesome," was far more conducive to moral well being than city life. Farming was a life of "much toil and exposure; yet few occupations seem so well suited to harmonize with our best feelings, or tend more to our preservation."[16] Removal to the country was prescribed for failing health, both physical and moral, and a stay in the country was sure to go a long way toward repairing the moral ravages of a "fashionable" upbringing.[17]

For all their endorsement of farm living, however, these

books seemed remote from its realities. A thoroughgoing depiction of a working farm, with horses, cows, pigs, chickens, fields, and work to be done at all hours, was rare indeed. Nowhere was there so much as a glimpse of the back-breaking kind of labor involved in farming before mechanization, such as Hamlin Garland detailed years later in *Boy Life on the Prairie*. Only the temperance tales revealed that it was standard custom in the period for a farmer to supply his harvest hands with whiskey during the long, hot days of harvesting.[18] In fact, only the temperance stories reveal that there *was* a harvest season. Such was the general pattern: unless there was a compelling didactic reason for including a specific of any kind, unless the detail contributed in some way to the spelling out of the message, the authors of juvenile tales usually dispensed with it.

As outdoors, so indoors. Mrs. Gaskell found American adult novels interesting for what they revealed about the daily ways of American life—"we see the meals as they are put on the table, we learn the dresses which those who sit down to them wear."[19] If she read them, she could not have found the children's books as interesting. Though the books were intensely domestic in their general atmosphere, there were few descriptions to make day-to-day domestic life vivid to a reader. Interiors were dismissed with as few words as were necessary to set the scene—they were "poor and bare," or "a single room, with little furniture in it," or "poor but clean"—unless they were Fashionable, in which case they were "richly furnished" or "imposing." Description of clothing was also largely an adjunct of moral didacticism. A wardrobe, like everything else, was to be "suited to [one's] circumstances, it was to be "plain, but neat, respectable and comfortable."[20] Morally correct clothing readily identified the fictional examples who wore it. "A pert-looking girl, about eleven years old, dressed in a fashionable frock, loaded with trimmings" was clearly not destined to be the heroine of the tale in which she appeared. Ann, whose "neat gingham dress" was regarded with scorn by the other girl, was on the right path.[21] More complete description of color, material, trim and style of clothing was omitted from most stories, the authors apparently considering an interest in such details too frivolous to satisfy.

The same austerity applied to matters of food. People in children's stories seldom ate, and when they did, the matter and the manner of their dinners were not often disclosed. What little discussion there was made it clear that food, like dress, should be simple. "To be sure, people must eat, in order to live," conceded Cardell, "but . . . eating is not the chief thing that they are to live for."[22] An 1830 story stressed the virtues of eating simply, and went on to point to God's wisdom and justice in "making an equality between the lot of the poor who love him and the Great who do not, by making plain bread taste as good as cake to those who live simply."[23] The distance between plain bread and cake is as close aś these stories came to revealing the differences in diet between rich and poor.

The absence of precise description was so nearly universal in these books as to make the exceptions stand out memorably. An 1859 story called *Bound Out*, by "Aunt Friendly," was an otherwise quite conventional little tale of Abby, an orphan, who was bound out at the age of ten to a farm family. The point of the story was not at all exceptional: Abby was the classic model of piety and moral rectitude who led the farmer and his wife back to Christian living, from which they had fallen away, and reformed their overindulgent handling of their little son, all by the silent power of example. The farm and its work were given as sketchily as ever; but indoors, the author, writing out of what was surely first-hand knowledge, gave glimpses of a whole rural way of living, including some of the contents of the pantry (a row of pies and a bowl of blackberries), what was served for breakfast (fried potatoes, ham and coffee), and even how it was eaten (with two-tined forks).[24]

Indeed, the thematic limitations and the overall blandness of the literature created a paradox: though American juvenile fiction developed in part out of the fervent nationalism of the period, it was often so narrowly focused and so closely modeled on its English predecessors that it is sometimes difficult to say with certainty that a given story is American rather than English. So firmly did the authors confine their interest to morality, conduct, and methods of nurture that in many books there was little, as least superficially, that was clearly American in background or ideology.[25]

The didacticism that dimmed the settings of most children's stories also flattened characterization. Since the characters in juvenile fiction existed solely to carry the moral message, they did not represent real people so much as kinds of behavior; they were models, in a fiction wholly given over to teaching, as the authors often said, "more by example than by precept." "Children learn much better from example than precept," observed the author of *Sarah and Her Cousins*. "They are, as all the world knows, most excellent imitators."[26]

Faith in the efficacy of example, including example set out rather baldly upon a printed page, was universal. "The development of the moral sentiments in the human heart, in early life," wrote Jacob Abbott, "is determined by sympathy, and by the influence of example."[27] William Cardell, whose *Story of Jack Halyard* was subtitled *The Virtuous Family*, forthrightly told parents and teachers in his preface that his purpose was "to give an account of one family of superior excellence, as a model to others."[28] No one questioned the idea that an example of superior excellence would spur others to emulation; it was a basic article of faith.

Moreover, the authors quite evidently hoped to encourage real children to become models of moral behavior for others in their own lives. They believed, with most of their contemporaries, in the power of an individual to affect greatly, for good or for ill, the lives of others, and they did not exclude children from the exercise of that power. "You occupy a place in society which no one else can fill," a fictional mother told her child.[29] Numbers of upright fictional children furnished helpful examples to less worthy fictional youth, and even the adults in children's stories were not beyond the reach of a good child. Though clearly it was not acceptable for a child to advise adults directly about their behavior, yet he could be an influence for good through the force of example. Abby, of *Bound Out*, achieved the ideal: "She had given no advice—she had but loved and lived as a Christian, and others had been led by her to seek the better way."[30]

Aside from George Washington, who was a constant model of character achieved, probably the best known good example of the period in children's books was that paragon of moral rectitude, Rollo, of Jacob Abbott's creation. Rollo was honest, trustworthy and high-minded, and always deeply concerned with the smallest gradations of moral judgment of his own thought and action. Yet he, like so many other child characters in these books, had little human dimension. Rollo did not laugh or doubt or fear or yearn except in moral terms. His strivings and failures, his lessons at school, his relations with other people all took place on the single plane of moral decision. And at that, Rollo was considerably more developed as a character than many a fictional child, simply by virtue of being hero of some twenty-eight stories.

The favored literary device for making the most of example —both good and bad—was that of contrast. American authors took over the method from their English predecessors in the field of didactic children's fiction—Maria Edgeworth is probably the best known among these—and used it enthusiastically, apparently convinced that the excellent qualities of good examples were set off to best advantage by strong contrast with the bad. Consequently, for every model of excellence in children's stories there was likely to be an example of mistake and misery meant to warn children of the ill effects of some particular character flaw.

However, it is a melancholy fact that goodness is less fascinating than badness, at least in literature. While good children of didactic fiction were often dull and unreal, the children whose faults were meant to furnish models of undesirable behavior sometimes achieved an authenticity lacking in their more virtuous counterparts. It was not that the authors treated their faulty examples with much more complexity than they brought to their models of excellence, but the first-hand knowledge of children that many of these authors had as parents and teachers sometimes seemed to assert itself when they dealt with childish faults and failings. Erratic and impulsive Laura, of *Laura's Impulses*, for instance, was a convincing picture of a warmhearted but unpersevering little girl who continually promised more good works than she was prepared to deliver. Laura was as much an example (of what to avoid) as all the other characters in juvenile stories, but her vows to be good-tempered, so quickly undone by a quarrel with her brother; her offer to teach some poor Irish children to read and her prompt disillusionment with their wigglesome and ungrateful ways; her promises to visit the house-bound sick, soon forgotten when something more interesting turned up—these were all very human and realistically childish.

Similarly, a bad girl named Dovey, in Abbott's *Rollo at School*, was a great deal more interesting that Rollo himself. Neglected and knocked about at home, taunted and disapproved abroad, Dovey was a classic case of defiantly aggressive behavior in school. And though Dovey was as wicked as she knew how to be—knocking over ink pots, running away from school, disobeying all kinds of rules, and openly defying the teacher—Abbott kept her behavior within the limits of believability. She was a realistic character, and quite pathetic.

There were other interestingly faulty children in the literature. No doubt the portraits of many of these imperfect but reformable children were drawn from life, while Rollo was the product of wishful thinking. Still, many of the bad examples were as flat and uninteresting as the good. Especially in the case of those bad examples who would not be reformed in the course of the story, but who would go directly to a disastrous but educational end, the characterization of bad children was often as overdrawn as that of the wholly good. Moreover, the reader's acquaintance with some of these models of ill-doing was so brief as to preclude any deep interest in their personalities. An indolent or a disobedient boy often hurtled from sin to sin with incredible dispatch, ending on the gallows or in a watery grave long before any fully dimensional literary portrait could possibly be achieved.

Adult characters were, if anything, even less developed than fictional children. They, too, were examples of behavior, ideal or not, and rarely had more than a single dimension. If ideal, adults were moral and rational—and perfect; there were no minor flaws or occasional lapses to mar the picture. The adults most frequently encountered in children's stories were, of course, parents, whose role in fiction was to provide models, both for adults who bought the books and possibly read them with their children, and for child readers who would surely grow up to take parental roles one day.

The ideal parent was well informed. He—or she, for women were as often the dispensers of endless information as men—could converse with ease and fluency on such varied topics as history, geography, geology, animal behavior, and the movements of the planets, and was perfectly prepared to do so at any moment. Fictional parents were also flawlessly rational; they never lost their tempers or their patience, and when the moment came for them to correct their children, they managed it without heat or anxiety. Emily, who was deliberately misbehaving, "looked in her mother's eyes but she discovered neither pity nor anger there," as her mother calmly administered the rational punishment that made Emily see the error of her way.[31]

Mothers figured more often in the stories than did fathers; the decision to give over the moral training of children to "the female hand" was faithfully reflected in most juvenile fiction. But, at least until the 1850s, fathers were not usually demoted by this maternal control. Sometimes father was the moral authority, guiding his family, dispensing knowledge and curbing the wayward. Even when he was a shadowy and distant figure, however, he was revered as husband and breadwinner. In *The Girl's Book*, Lydia Sigourney presented the ideal mother as a woman of "serious dignity," who taught her daughter "all the necessary employments," and especially "to consider the interests of their father as their own, and instructed them by her own example how to lessen his expenses." In this way, Mrs. Sigourney explained, his children "are capital, whose value increases every year. . . . If he incurs misfortune, they join and help him out."[32] But it was quite typical that this fortunate father played no part in the story, and that it was the mother's moral teaching that permeated the household.

Imperfect adults, like imperfect children, were mostly display cases for one ruinous fault. As the ideal adult was never shown as having a few small failings, so the fallen adult had few redeeming virtues. The most disastrous flaw in a fictional husband and father was a weakness for drink. The drunkard was a familiar character in children's books, who was by no means confined to temperance tracts. He visited the consequences of his addiction on families high and low throughout the literature, wreaking havoc with the hopes, the feelings, and the fortunes of his wife and children. Only the death or desertion of a father was as great a tragedy for his dependents. Though drink was not the only failing attributed to grown men in children's tales, it was overwhelmingly the major one until late in the period. Perhaps lesser frailties were forgiven if they did not interfere with a man's main function as a provider.

Women in children's fiction had slightly more range for their faults. In their role as mothers, they might fail by being neglectful of their children, or "yielding" toward them, or "fashionable," or any combination of these. As wives, they might fail their husbands by being fashionable; that is, extravagant, fretful and shallow, unable or unwilling to deal constructively with daily problems or with reverse of fortune. Or, they might be ill-educated in their duties and, thus, incapable of managing a household efficiently and economically. This latter fault might be, and often was, one of the many drawbacks of being fashionable, but sometimes it was the failing of one who was really good at heart, only badly or too intellectually educated.[33]

Women who were selfish and indolent, who were given to novel-reading or to vanity—all those described so oddly by Mrs. Sigourney as "effeminate"—were a disaster to themselves, their families, and even to their country. ("Indolence and effeminacy are peculiarly unfit for the daughters of a republic," remarked Mrs. Sigourney.)[34] They indulged their children "through selfish love of ease,"[35] and thereby ruined their characters and, in due time, their lives.[36] They could not or would not teach their servants their proper tasks and direct them with the necessary firmness and tact, so that their households were disorderly and unpleasant even when wealthy, and they fell to pieces altogether when misfortune struck.[37] Of course, such mothers could not provide their children with the example or the guidance so needful for a child's moral development, and so, although some of their offspring miraculously escaped the fate of the badly reared child (often through the intervention of a more worthwhile relative), many more fell by the way-side—idle, selfish, irresolute, sometimes drunken and criminal as well.[38]

Fashionableness was the fault in women most comparable to that of drunkenness in men, since it had the same effect of making them unfit for their highest duties. It was defined only by implication, but it clearly stood for an entire value system wrongly based. A woman who was "a slave to [Fashion's] absurdities and every changing temperament" had none of the inner resources necessary for successful management of her responsiblities as wife and mother.[39] Her position was deplorable, for "there is no slavery so irksome, as that which people bring on themselves, when they have no other criterion for right or wrong than the opinion of others."[40] For the authors of children's books in this period, there was scarcely a greater womanly failing than Fashionableness, and they never used the word but with the utmost scorn.

There was never a problem in identifying these faulty adults, nor in knowing how their shortcomings would be repaid. Except for the occasional well-intentioned but ill-trained wife and mother who might be reformed by a more exemplary woman, one fault generally implied the rest of the story. A woman of Fashion was always a hopeless case; she neglected home and children and husband until all was in ruins about her. A mother characterized as indolent was never redeemed by her good nature or by an ability to tell stories or bake cakes. A drunkard might reform under the proper influence, but he was much more likely to die of drink. It was certain that he would not be allowed by any children's author to live on, sometimes drunk, sometimes decent—an equivocal, complex human being. Examples cannot have aspects and complexities; they must be clear and unmistakable, and so they always were in children's stories.

Simplicity of characterization and absence of specific and detailed description contributed to a curious sense of isolation that ran all through the books of children's fiction in the period. The stories seemed to take place in a vacuum, or at least in some very generalized locale, and the characters were only rarely convincingly drawn human figures. There was an "eventless" feeling to the narratives that resulted less from a real absence of incident than from the thinness of the authors' literary treatment of time, place, and people.

A sense of isolation prevailed within the stories as well. In most tales, the circle of personal life was drawn very small. Large families were a rarity in these books; in a typical story, there were one to three children at home, seldom more. The usual household was limited, moreover, to what modern parlance calls the nuclear family—that is, to mother, father, and children. The extended family of several generations under one roof, often supposed to be typical of American families before the twentieth century, was decidedly not the family pictured in the children's fiction of the time. Sometimes a grandmother was part of a household, and aunts and uncles might come to visit or be close enough to be visited, but the most commonly shown situation was that of parents and children living of and to themselves.[41]

That this picture was generally accurate for the period was suggested by one author who described a three-generation household, and remarked upon the virtue of this arrangement over the "deserted old age, which from the eager pursuit of independence is too common among us."[42] Her "eager pursuit of independence" was one of the many oblique references in children's stories to the great physical expansion which did indeed separate the generations as young people left the villages where they grew up to make their homes and found their own families in newly opened territories or in cities. If the restless mobility of Americans in the early nineteenth century was rarely the subject of children's stories, its effects were, nevertheless, everywhere between the lines.

To family isolation was added a larger social isolation. Very little sense of community was projected through these tales; no more than the most rudimentary comprehension of the social structure of town or village can be gleaned from them, and little feeling for how life was lived outside the home. Persons other than family had small place in the lives of fictional children, though teachers figured in some stories, playing roles very similar to those of parents in providing education heavily moral in emphasis. Sunday Schools were important to some tales, not necessarily only those published by the Sunday School societies.[43] In general, however, the institutions of society were all but invisible. Schools were remarkably nondescript in a literature written for children, social affairs outside the home went unmentioned, and even churches, in books altogether pervaded by religious morality, played almost no institutional part in the lives of people in the stories. Small as it was, the domestic circle encompassed most of the concerns of children's fiction. The loneliness that was the unacknowledged companion of individualism and middle-class family life haunted the fictional tales of families who seemed to have few close and necessary ties to their communities.

But if the world in children's fiction was narrow, flat, and often featureless, it nevertheless contained a number of realities since banished from much of children's literature. While some stories dealt only in childish concerns—school rivalries, minor acts of disobedience with minor consequences, and the like—many more faced their child protagonists with the starkest of calamities. The death of parents occurred often in the stories, and poverty was even more common; disease, sin, and moral failure were acknowledged realities in the lives of all people, including children, and were standard elements in the literature. In fact, the overall picture of human life was deeply shadowed by uncertainty; the world as glimpsed in children's fiction was threatening, however hazy, and the cumulative message to child readers was a warning. For good reason, stories like these have been called cautionary tales.

A major theme of the books was the impermanence of life, fortune, and happiness. Young readers were continually reminded that there was no lasting happiness here below and that "many things, such as youth, beauty, pleasure and riches, are almost as fleeting as the rainbow; and though they may please us for a time, yet they vanish and appear no more."[44] Appearances are deceptive, the books taught; "it often happens, that what is pleasant to the eye, is full of danger; and young people should take care how they are enticed by mere beauty."[45] Achievements and glory were also fleeting: "Our learning may gain applause, and make us useful. But we cannot tell how soon all which belongs to the earth, shall lie mouldering with its kindred dust."[46] The counsel one fictitious child received from her dying mother was that of most stories: "Expect trouble always," the mother advised, "and make up your mind to bear it."[47]

And indeed, disaster struck often and fatefully in the literature. Sudden financial reverses were common. Even families of moderate wealth found themselves plunged overnight into straightened circumstances, their resources of character and skill taxed to the utmost to repair economic damages against which, apparently, there was little protection. The economic uncertainties of the period, which were certainly very real —as severe depressions in 1819, 1837 and 1857 testified—appeared in the literature in a form characteristically reduced to personal terms.

The causes behind economic reverses were generally left unexplored in the fiction; what was told was how the family members responded to the challenge of adversity. The tales usually dealt in pairs of families, to allow for an instructive comparison of right and wrong responses. *The Contrast*, for instance, presents two cousins, Susan and Amelia, whose attitudes toward work, wealth, and poverty—set out at the beginning of the narrative, when both households are well off —make perfectly clear which is better equipped to handle misfortune. Amelia discusses the unpredictability of fortune with Susan: "Mother says, rich people often lose their property . . . and become poor." Therefore, Amelia explains, it is mother's advice that everyone, prosperous or not, should learn the "useful arts." The effort cannot be wasted in any event, since even if one never needs it oneself, such knowledge "might be useful in affording assistance to others who are poor and industrious."[48] However, Susan scorns useful work and, even worse, she is snobbish and aloof from those less fortunate than herself; she acts "as if riches and pride, rather than virtue and industry, formed the standard by which we are to estimate true greatness."[49]

The attitudes of the two girls reflect faithfully the maternal influence on each, making predictable their response to adversity. ("How important then is the culture of the female mind!")[50] Each family loses its fortune, and the mothers react in characteristic ways. Susan's mother, selfish and fond of ease, cannot adjust. She remains idle, broods over her misfortunes, falls ill and dies. Amelia's mother, on the other hand, is serene and rational. She is able to get along without servants, since she is, herself, well versed in the household arts and has trained her daughter in them as well. Even when her husband dies, she is able to meet the occasion with inner strength. In strict accord with the philosophy of the literature, the daughters are products of their home training, and so face this trial of character as their mothers have fitted them to do. Susan succumbs to discouragement, while Amelia meets the tests with practical skills and moral courage.

In stories like this, the level of poverty to which the characters were reduced, though it was none too clearly described, was plainly something less than desperate. The family usually had to leave a fine house in town, give up their servants (or all but one), and move into the country. But the "modest" homes to which they removed were by no means hovels, and there was certainly no question of starvation. Usually, too, the family fortunes recovered to some extent before the end of the tale.

However, truly desperate poverty did appear in much of the fiction; and if the financial misfortunes of the wealthy were accounted for sketchily or not at all in most of the books, the case was very different for people of lesser means. The cause of real destitution was always the same—always it was the loss of the family breadwinner. The widow and the orphan stand forth in all their helplessness in the children's fiction before 1860. Their poverty was not merely genteel; the loss of the family provider through death, drink, or desertion often left women and children exposed to real privation. With few means of earning a living open to them, they faced homelessness and hunger. When this happened—and it was remarkably frequent in these stories —the sense of isolation so characteristic of the literature crystallized into a stark phrase used over and over by the authors: the destitute victims of circumstance were "thrown upon the cold charity of the world." Nothing is more striking in the many stories that deal with poverty than the authors' insistence that the only real recourse for the desperately needy was the charity of individuals, and that that charity was uncertain at best.[51]

Samuel Goodrich, for instance, in a tale for quite young children, told a brief but bleak story of an Irish boy brought to America by his "poor but honest" father after his mother's death in Ireland. For a while they get along well enough, with the father working as a gardener; but soon the father dies, leaving the little boy entirely on his own. "He was very young, and now, alas! he was destitute of everything." When he is very hungry, the boy goes out into the street, finds the house of a rich man and asks in the kitchen for food. "But the woman had a hard heart, and would give him nothing. . . . In vain did the little boy plead for a single crust of bread." He is sent out into the street again, hungry and cold. In due time, and in accordance with the general pattern of such tales, the child is found and adopted by a benevolent Christian—apparently the only kind of rescue available to him.[52]

Another very brief tale in verse, entitled *The Child of Want and Misery*, did little more than outline the plight of an impoverished child. Two little girls meet an orphaned boy. His father "went for a soldier" and was killed, his mother "died of sorrow," and he is reduced to poverty—not quite begging, but dependent nevertheless upon the charity of others. The little girls each give him a pence "to help ease his pain," and that is the end of the story.

These stories were entirely typical and were paralleled many times in the literature. The main elements—the death of the father, the breadwinner; the destitution of the child, with or without his mother; the dependence upon the charity of individuals; and the uncertainty of receiving that charity—were used over and over in children's fiction of the period.

Very infrequently, there was an indication that some community resources for the care of the poor did exist, but during most of the period these institutions were dismissed quickly, leaving the impression that they were not only the last but the worst refuge for the desperate. In C. M. Sedgwick's *Stories for Young Persons*, a woman whose children were near starvation still considered any struggle preferable to dependence on public charity, "for that . . . was what nobody took pleasure in giving, and no one was thankful for receiving."[53] In *Mary Wilson, A Tale of New England*, the author remarked of an ill-treated bound-out boy that "the town was not particular enough who they bind their poor to," suggesting that town-supported care was both heartless and offhand.[54] Churches were simply never mentioned as a source of aid to the poor.

There were certainly realities behind these stark pictures. Community arrangements for the care of the helpless and the destitute were at best very sketchy in this period; at worst, they were appallingly unsatisfactory, as David Rothman has shown in *The Discovery of Asylum*.[55] Moreover, the pressures of expansion and mobility tended to break up a sense of community and dilute the traditional notion that the community should "take care of its own." If the old system of binding out could be cruel, the charity of individuals was likely to be cold indeed where those who had enough to spare neither knew nor felt responsible for those in need. Hostility toward cities often centered on the charge that it was all too easy to be uncaring toward the needs of others in a city.[56] And some of the fervor on the part of these authors when they described the helplessness of widows and orphans can surely be traced to personal experience. A number of women authors had themselves been widowed while their children were still young.[57] Though it is unlikely that any of them were entirely without family resources, still they must have had ample opportunity to recognize how few alternatives to charity were available to women in their society. With no great imaginative effort, they must have been able to understand the desperate position of a woman who had to support herself and her children with few skills and fewer opportunities for employment.

Like poverty, death was a common feature in the children's fiction before 1860; children were schooled to consider life itself as the least certain of blessings. The literature was studded with reflections upon the brevity of human life, and the consequent wisdom of making the spiritual most of the time available. Norman and his mother, gazing at the mighty falls of Niagara, were moved to observe how "truly, there is but a step between us and death," and when they heard the story of two young people who lost their lives there, Norman's mother pointed out "how many are daily and hourly borne, by the mighty tides of worldliness and sin, over a more tremendous precipice."[58]

The death of a parent, sometimes of both parents, formed the dramatic base of many tales, which then went on to relate how the children coped with their situation, bereft of the guidance and protection of a parent's care. The frequency with which this one simple plot was used suggests how convenient it was for displaying the moral lessons the authors wanted to convey. The importance of parental love and protection was dramatized by its loss; the importance of parental teaching was demonstrated by how well the orphaned child was able to manage his own. The Christian obligation to practice charity was given point by picturing the desperate straits of an orphaned and helpless child.

Children were not exempt from death in the literature for the young. The children of nineteenth-century fiction did not die quite so frequently as those of eighteenth-century literature, but a child's death was a familiar event in the stories. And here the authors' claim to realism was upheld by statistics. High child mortality was a fact of the period, and few children growing up before 1860 reached maturity without experiencing the death of a brother or sister or child acquaintance.[59] What was a commonplace in life was not filtered out of the fiction. Young readers were often reminded that for them, as for adults, death was "always near" and that they must be conscious always of their "readiness for the next world." Such reminders were, of course, frequently employed to underpin didactic messages; the brevity of life and the swiftness of time were reasons to think seriously on the moral conduct of the hour.[60]

But child mortality was also recorded, simply and sadly, as a fact of human life, and somehow the philosophy offered to children had to account for this, as for happier evidences of God's will. The standard comfort was the assurance that the dead child had gone to a better world, where he would be happy and free of pain. In its best expression, this philosophy carried the conviction of perfect faith. Mrs. Cheseboro's *Smiles and Tears*, which was largely a reminiscence of her own childhood, recounted an episode probably quite characteristic for the era. In one chapter of the book, a little girl in town died of a "brain fever." Her young friends brought flowers, viewed the body, and attended the funeral. In the telling, at least, the experience was neither morbid nor sentimental; the children were assured that Fanny was "happier in heaven" and that when she is buried, it will not be Fanny herself, but only "the garment of the soul" which is put in the earth.

Now and then, the surface calm of this outlook cracked a little to show the grief below. The short and stiffly written little tale of *Blind Susan* told how Susan's cataracts were successfully removed, to the joy of her "affectionate family." But soon after the operation, she "drooped" and declined and, in a little while, died. The special sense of loss at a child's death shines through the conventional rhetoric in the author's comment: "Death comes to the aged like a reaper to . . . ripe grain, but to the young it comes like the scythe of the mower which cuts down the flower." After this, however, there was a swift return to the reassurance that Susan was happier "taken from this dark world to enjoy true felicity in the courts of her God."[62]

The death of a child was always explained this way. Some stories suggest that children did not always find it easy to reconcile the death of a good child with what they were told about God's love for good children. Nellie Russell asked about the death of a pious child: Did not God love little Susan Ward? She was assured he did. "But isn't it very strange, then, that he should let her get sick and die?" To which her aunt replied, "It may seem strange to you, Nellie, who do not know what a beautiful place heaven is, and what a happy home it has been to Susan. . . . Angels must have considered it as the greatest blessing that could have happened to a little girl like her to be placed so soon where she would never suffer from sin, or sickness, or pain of any kind."[63]

Nellie was, of course, satisfied with this answer, but other books confirmed the impression that her doubts were by no means uncommon. Early children's books, especially those of the eighteenth century, contained so many holy deaths of good children that apparently some of their readers fell under the misapprehension that the wages of virtue were death. An 1845 Sunday School Union book undertook to combat the "settled opinion" among children that the good die early by assuring readers that it was misbehavior rather than goodness that killed most children.[64]

In spite of the prevalence of death in the stories, however, and in spite of the authors' undeniable efforts to engage the sympathies of their readers for the orphaned child and the widowed mother, the literary handling of death in children's fiction was, for the most part, surprisingly unsentimental. At a time when adult popular fiction abounded in drawn-out, harrowing deathbed scenes, the same scenes in children's stories were usually treated briefly and matter-of-factly. Early in the period there were, to be sure, some of the lingering accounts of holy and happy deaths typical of eighteenth-century children's tales, but these were relatively rare after 1830. In the '30s and '40s especially, practical considerations generally overrode the emotional aspects of death.

One of Jacob Abbott's *Franconia Tales*, for example, told of a young woman whose husband had fallen ill. "Mary Erskine stood leaning over him for some time, with a countenance filled with anxiety and concern. She then turned away, saying to herself, 'If Albert is going to be sick and die, what *will* become of me?' " Abbott also avoided an affecting deathbed scene, remarking merely that "stories of sickness and suffering are painful to read. . . . We will therefore shorten the tale of Mary Erskine's anxiety and distress, by saying at once that Albert grew worse instead of better, every day for a fortnight, and then died."[65] In very similar words, the author of *Adelaide* bypassed the sentimental possibilities of a mother's death: "I shall pass over this scene and continue the story of Adelaide—only remarking that they deeply felt and mourned their loss. But they knew it was God who had ordered the event."[66]

Even those stories that treated death with a bit more drama than this avoided, for the most part, the deathbed promises extracted and reforms exacted common to sentimental fiction for adults. In contrast to later books, the children in juvenile fiction of this period did not usually convert and reform as they died—they just died. "She closed her eyes, and in a few minutes afterwards, her spirit fled—none knew whither—but it was gone! The body was indeed there; but it was not Mary Wilson. Perhaps Mary herself was already with the angels as she hoped to be."[67]

In general, juvenile fiction supported an attitude of acceptance toward death. While the authors certainly acknowledged the pain of bereavement, they neither portrayed nor, apparently, approved excessive expressions of grief. Death was an expression of God's will, and uncontrolled grief was a kind of rebellion.

Mrs. Sedgewick's *Moral Tales* included an unusual story of a clergyman visiting a woman "who murmured very much, on account of a serious misfortune—the loss of a child." The clergyman said all he could to console her, "but in vain; she was still loud in her murmuring. . . . He, at length, became quite indignant. 'Well, Madam,' said he, 'God has seen fit, in his holy providence, to take away your child; and what do you propose to do about it?' "[68] It is impossible to know from context whether this curious tale was meant to be amusing or instructive or both, but the attitude was typical, if the statement was more blunt than most. In another story, a young girl's mother made clear to her daughter how the impending death of her father was to be taken. When Ella asked, "May we not grieve for him when he is gone?" her mother answered, "All grief is, in the abstract, selfish."[69]

The correct attitude was unmistakably identified in many stories. The tale of *The Morton Family*, which amounted to little more than a narrative of the deaths, one by one, of an entire family, provided ample demonstration. Early in the story, the son of the family, whose besetting sin is uncontrolled outbursts of anger, threatens his sister with a shotgun he believes to be unloaded. She, who is herself less than perfect in loving kindness and humility, still refuses to do what he is asking, and he pulls the trigger. Ann falls to the floor, fatally wounded but cured of her own selfishness, and uttering forgiveness of her brother with her last breath. Such a tragedy might well be expected to leave the mother of these unfortunate young people prostrate with grief, but Mrs. Morton was created to provide a model of Christian acceptance for young readers: "It would seem as if this blow would have been almost overwhelming to Mrs. Morton, but she was a Christian, not in name only, but in practice." Mrs. Morton finds it possible not only to contain her grief, but to be thankful it was Ann rather than Edward who had died, since he is still so unready for death. Her remaining children grasp the principle so well that when Mrs. Morton herself dies somewhat later in the story, "Charles and Eliza viewed with some composure the remains of one who had so well fulfilled the responsible office of a parent." In accordance with the general philosophy of this and many other juvenile tales, the author noted that "it would be the extreme of selfishness to wish to recall her to a world where she had suffered so much."[70]

Poverty and death were only the most extreme of the hazards common in children's fiction. There were many other afflictions, from physical ailments of various kinds and degrees to moral failures large and small, adult as well as childish. Disease was ever present in stories (as in reality) and much feared. Though the families of children's fiction nearly always seemed to have doctors available to call, their practical efficacy was doubtful. Almost any ailment was likely to be fatal, and the doctor's role often seemed to be confined to offering his opinion on the probability of recovery. Parents of fictional children were anxiously cautious about matters of physical health. Little Susie of a *Juvenile Miscellany* story, when she was drenched in a spring rain, was not just dried off and given a change of clothing, but put to bed for the rest of the day to prevent her taking cold. Frederick, of *Conquest and Self-Conquest*, spent three weeks in bed with a broken arm. Susie's mother, in *Self-Willed Susie*, entreated her daughters to stay home for a proposed walk on a summer day: "I think there is real danger that you will get sick if you do it in such extremely warm weather."[71]

Nor did the uncertainties surrounding the child of juvenile fiction end with the material and physical. He had also to reckon with the moral failings of adults, sometimes of his own parents. Later children's books have subscribed nearly unanimously to the convention that parents are the firm center in a child's life. If not wholly perfect (and often it has been implied that they are), parents have rarely been shown as the cause of a child's troubles. Until very recently, an alcoholic parent or a deserting father or a shallow, lazy mother was virtually taboo in children's stories. But the fiction written for children before 1860, while it frequently went further than any modern literature in embellishing the portrait of the perfect father or mother, also admitted the existence of those who were less—sometimes much less—than perfect. The drunken father, that staple of temperance literature—children's as well as adult—also appeared in many books not otherwise specifically "temperance." Sometimes a fictional father seems to have abandoned his family for reasons left unexplained; and sometimes, especially in stories written late in this period, fathers were criticized for neglecting their families in their preoccupation with money-making.[72]

While motherhood could be a state as close to sainthood as mortally possible, neglectful or selfish mothers were certainly very common in the books. There were sharp comments on mothers whose indulgence of their children was more a matter of lazy indifference to their welfare than of love, and on those whose lack of firm moral standards undermined all discipline, to the ultimate detriment of their children's characters and careers.

Children could hardly be warned against their own parents, but they were nevertheless strenuously educated by the authors of their fiction on the traits of bad as well as good parental behavior. In a more general way, they were warned against the possible untrustworthiness of other human beings: "Never take the advice of those who are known to be deceitful and treacherous," advised Samuel Goodrich in his *Book of Fables,* and, "when a known enemy wishes to seem a friend, there is most cause for us to keep out of his reach."[73] Very little in this literature encouraged a child to view either the world or its inhabitants through rose-colored glasses. Kindness and benevolence were highly-prized virtues in the stories, but they were not depicted as universal, no more among the adult characters than amongst the children. From the "hard-hearted" woman who refused the little Irish boy's request, to the New York alderman indifferent to an orphaned boy's need for help and guidance in a strange city, adults were shown as morally varied and often imperfect—as was, indeed, the world. "Alas, almost everything in this world is imperfect and incomplete," lamented the author of *Self-Willed Susie.*[74]

Taken all in all, the external reality pictured for children by their fiction was far from reassuring. It was vague, yet threatening; dim, but full of danger. Not even in their literature were children exempted from the hazards of life; indeed, the fiction seemed often specifically designed to remind the young that life could be as harsh for them as for adults. Far from seeking to assure children of the safety of their childhood years, authors pointed out the pitfalls of human existence insistently, warning their happiest readers that fortune was fleeting and life uncertain, and that no man—or child—knew what the morrow might bring.

Nor was the human society that surrounded a growing child portrayed as a reliable source of help in time of trouble. The concept of community was blurred in the stories; institutions played no certain role in the life of an individual. Charity, though praiseworthy, was purely voluntary and could be neither claimed nor relied upon with certainty. The few descriptions of community resources available to the needy were so darkened by distaste and disapproval that no child reader could have taken heart from them.

Even the home, that citadel of good constantly celebrated in the period, could offer only limited protection to a child against the outer world. Home was not proof against sickness, death or poverty, and the greatest tragedies, like drunkenness and moral failure, were horrifying precisely because they invaded and destroyed family and home.

Yet the books were not written to frighten children away from taking part in society. No writer envisioned his young audience growing into some sheltered class of adults who would or could keep clear of the social and personal dangers the stories warned of. On the contrary, it was clear in every line that the fiction was written to prepare a generation soon to be active in the affairs of a democratic country, and the version of reality presented in the stories was meant to contribute to that end.

Not art, but outlook shaped these tales. The distortions, the omissions, the characteristic imbalance between inner and outer experience, were all products of the authors' angle of vision.

Writers included in their juvenile books those aspects of life they believed children must know and understand, both for their own protection and for the sake of American society. From their point of view, what they told children *was* realistic, and would serve to prepare them for their encounter with the world. If the world they pictured in fiction was dangerous, it was because they believed that the real world was indeed dangerous for the unprepared. If the accounts of physical and social reality were vague, it was because most of these authors saw significant experience in moral rather than physical or social terms. The single most vivid element in every tale was the moral lesson, for the very good reason that morality seemed at once the quality most necessary to the survival of the Republic and most threatened by the competitive, shifting realities of American life.

The home training idealized in the fiction never offered to teach children how to manipulate the outer environment to insure their happiness or success. Quite the contrary; it suggested that they could hope for little control over circumstance and that they must therefore learn to be independent of events, as far as possible. Children were steadily warned against looking for fulfillment in wealth and worldly praise. These were too fragile, too unreliable, too difficult to attain and hold to make it wise to base one's happiness upon them. For all the noisy rhetoric about success and opportunity rampant in the period, most juvenile fiction was as concerned to prepare its readers for failure as for success. All children, rich as well as poor, girls as well as boys, were urged to develop practical skills that would enable them to manage in the face of financial adversity. All children were told by their books that contentment was neither a product nor a victim of outer reality, but of inner character. Whatever else he found in these stories, the child who read them could scarcely have failed to understand that he must seek his security, not in the outer world, but within his own heart, and that his capacity to deal with an unreliable universe was wholly dependent upon the strength of the moral character he developed in his growing years.

III

"Those Excellent Children"

In the brief span of years that made up his childhood, an American child had to learn the principles, form the character, and acquire the moral strength that would enable him to deal successfully with a future at once promising and threatening. His books were most earnestly dedicated to helping him in this formidable task, most soberly devoted to teaching the virtues indispensable to human happiness and security. What, then, did they teach? Which were the qualities the authors of children's fiction thought would enable children to cope with the uncertain world beyond the home? In stories written to hold up to children an ideal example for imitation, who was an ideal child?

The story of *Little Mary* was written, the subtitle says, "for children from four to five years old." The narrative follows Mary through a day or so of her life with her calm, rational parents who are fully committed to the task of molding their daughter into an ideal child.

Chapter 1 begins with a dialogue between Mary and her mother. Mother tells Mary that she has a headache and is going to go upstairs to lie down. Mary asks to go with her, promising to play quietly enough not to disturb mother. Soon after mother falls asleep, father comes in and invites Mary to come downstairs with him; but Mary thinks she must keep her promise and stay, though her mother is asleep. When mother wakes, she and Mary discuss this decision: Was Mary right to stay? Yes, her mother tells her, because one must keep one's promises. Would she have been wicked to go downstairs with her father? No, because she had not promised not to go down, yet it had been her choice to come up and "you must always abide by your choice." If she had made a noise, *then* she would have been wicked, "for then you would have told a falsehood." And, as noise might have resulted had she gone downstairs, she was right to stay. When Mary does finally go downstairs to see Papa, there is much further discussion of whether she has been good or not. Papa gives her flowers because she has been good. Mary says she is "always happier" when she is good.[1]

On the following day, while Mary and her mother are going to visit Susan, the daughter of a "poor, but very good woman," Mary falls, dirtying her dress and hurting her hand. She does not cry, though she tells her mother "I felt as if I should." "No, my love," replies her mother, "I hope not; it is very childish to cry at every little hurt."[2]

Along the way, Mary and her mother see a white lamb, which enchants Mary. She wants to take it home with her, but her mother instructs her otherwise: "To take the property of another, even a very small thing, is stealing, and that is very wicked." Home again, Mary runs to tell her father about the visit, but her mother halts her. First, Mary must put her outer clothing away neatly upstairs. Then she joins her parents for supper, but "as she was never allowed to talk at table, she ate her supper, but did not speak." When supper is over, Mary's father at last asks her about her outing. There is a final catechism on behavior before bedtime. "Come," says mother. "Come sit with me and tell me if you have been a good girl all day." Mary says quickly that she has been, but mother says, "Think . . . before you answer." Mary thinks, and admits to having been cross with her kitty—striking her when she scratched. "But, Mary," says her father, "does your mother strike you every time you are naughty?" "No, Papa," replies Mary, "Mama hardly ever takes the rod, only sometimes when I am very, very naughty." "How does she punish you when you do wrong?" "Mama will not talk with me, or tell me stories, or kiss me, and sometimes she puts me behind her chair; and then I am so sorry, I think I will never be a naughty girl again." But Mary goes on to say that such methods wouldn't work with kitty. Her parents agree, but they tell her to be gentle and amiable, for "if you are rough and cross to your kitten, I am afraid you will be cross to the little girls at school, and then they will not love you." At the end of this discussion, Mary goes to bed, and the tale is also at an end.[3]

The story of *Little Mary* told a good deal (as, indeed, it was meant to) about both the character and the training of an ideal child. The basic tenets of her upbringing—restraint, self-control, and a concept of happiness based on a conviction of moral goodness—were perfectly clear and were among those overwhelmingly endorsed by the children's books of the period. Her training in these qualities was already well under way at an early age. Mary was presumably as young as the intended audience for her story, yet she was subject to a discipline that was constant and strict, though it was also loving. Her spontaneous reactions were continually curbed and channeled; a high degree of self-discipline was expected of her despite her youth.

One significant element in Mary's upbringing was the extent to which she, herself, was involved in it. Mary was very much a party to her own training; she was steadily encouraged to examine rather closely both the nature of goodness and her own behavior, and the story showed her doing this with some interest and anxiety. Such an approach to child nurture clearly gave point to a didactic literature whose function it was to provide examples and standards against which a child reader could measure his own performance.

The purpose of Mary's careful training was that of all ideal child training in the period—the right development of character. The concept of character at this time in the nineteenth century was, as William Taylor has pointed out, normative rather than descriptive.[4] It encompassed those qualities vital in the home nurture of Mary and all other well brought up children, that is, restraint, self-control, self-discipline—self-denial, in fact, to an extraordinary degree—and thus set the goals toward which an ideal child must strive.

The emphasis in children's fiction of the period upon the concept of character can scarcely be overstated; it was central to every story written. Character was the object of a child's education and the subject of every moral discourse. A good character was the cornerstone of all achievement, the foundation of every success. Sterling character was far more lauded in the fiction than intelligence, talent, or skill; George Washington, who was celebrated endlessly throughout the literature, was praised, not for his military accomplishments nor his presidential or administrative abilities, but for his "noble character."

Broadly speaking, the scheme of moral values which undergirded the concept of good character had two poles, selflessness and selfishness. Around one clustered all virtue; around the other, most vice. The noblest aims of human life and the source of all human happiness were to be found in self-denial. Conversely, nearly all human failing was attributed to selfishness in one form or another. The aim of all proper character development was to inculcate the virtues which came under the general heading of selflessness and to prevent or to eradicate the heinous fault of selfishness. The training of an ideal child, then, opposed "self-will" in every form, holding out to children the promise of that rarified happiness which comes only to those who have mastered the difficult art of self-discipline.

The deep seriousness of children's stories turned upon the authors' conviction that early training was vital to the right development of a child's character. The child was father to the man: "Bring a child up in the way he should go, and he will not depart from it when he is a man." Good habits were the building blocks of good character, and they could not be established too early—as little Mary's parents so evidently believed. Good habits were not easy to acquire, but they were moral surety against future temptation. Bad habits, on the other hand, were all too quickly learned, and only slowly and with great difficulty unlearned: "Not in a moment my character underwent a change," confided a reformed rake to his young listener. "It was the work of years."[5]

A diligent parent watched his children carefully, and never allowed a bad habit to grow unchecked where a good should bloom. One careful father who had observed that his little daughter played when she should have been studying, called her in for a talk. Her conduct was a sin, her father explained to her, because to keep on so would surely form "habits of idleness, listlessness, loitering, and self-indulgence, instead of diligence, perseverance and resolution."[6]

Good habits made good character, and character alone could guarantee happiness in this world and the next. Lydia Maria Child spoke for all her fellow writers when she exclaimed fervently, "Oh, if I could impress upon the young the vast importance of the habits they form in early life! The characters you are now forming are to make you happy, or unhappy for—Eternity!"[7]

In the litany of good habits these books sought to inculcate, obedience was the first law of life. The author of a tale published in *The Juvenile Miscellany* established the whole character of a seven-year-old boy in her remark that he was "one of those excellent children, who always think the judgment of their parents superior to their own."[8] Mrs. Sigourney told her young readers, "Next to your duty to God, is your duty to your parents," and added firmly that it was "not necessary" that a child understand "the reason of their commands."[9] Though, in fact, the mothers and fathers in children's fiction explained their commands to their children at considerable length, it was not theoretically required that they do so, for parental authority, as Mrs. Bradley pointed out in *Douglass Farm*, was "God's word" to children.[10]

More commonly, however, the argument for obedience to parents was not from religious authority so much as from the sentiment a child should bear toward his parents. The authors of children's fiction could scarcely frame statements strong enough to convey to children how much reverence and gratitude they owed their parents. "The obligation on the side of children to their parents can never be acquitted," thought one writer, who devoted an entire book to *Filial Duty Recommended and Enforced, by a Variety of Instructive and Amusing Narratives.*[11] Indeed, some of the amusing and instructive narratives did suggest that there were no limits to the demands of filial affection. In one anecdote, an eight-year-old child of extremely poor parents "stripped himself naked to the waist and stood by the side of [their] bed, exposing his delicate skin to the flies, without driving them away. 'When they are filled with my blood,' said he, 'they will let my parents be at rest.' "[12] Such a story was atypical, certainly, but the basic sentiment was not. In another, less morbid story, a young girl vowed to "live a life of love and devotion to her mother," and it was clear that the author found this an admirable ambition.[13]

The authors did not hesitate to encourage children in their filial loyalties by whatever means were at hand; they often reminded their readers that parents could die, and that a disobedient or ungrateful child's grief would be sharpened by the memory of his shortcomings. In a gentle story titled *Childhood*, the author wrote, "Little children, who have kind fathers and mothers, cannot be too thankful to God for them. They cannot be too careful to obey them, and try to make them happy. If their father or mother should die, they would be very sorry that they had ever disobeyed them, or done anything to grieve or trouble them."[14] Mrs. Sigourney, too, recommended that children consider the miseries of orphanage while they were blessed with living parents and "never be so ungrateful as to distress them by disobedience."[15]

That a child's obedience to his parents had more than domestic significance was clear. Mrs. Sigourney and the author of *Filial Duty* were agreed that "the obedience of children to their parents is the basis of all government."[16] Lydia Sigourney told children to "take pleasure in obeying the commands of your superiors," and pointed out to them how important it was that all authority be honored: "If in nations, the laws were disregarded, what safety would there be for the people?" She wanted children to "shew respect to magistrates, and to all who are in places of authority. There would be fewer mutinies and revolutions, if children were trained up in obedience." And with doubtful logic, she cited the example of Washington, whose "first lesson was to obey."[17]

Exhortations to children to obey their parents were buttressed by tales of awful consequences to those who disobeyed. "Disobedience is generally punished in some way or other," warned Samuel Goodrich, "and often very severely."[18] "The number of children who die from the effects of disobedience to their parents is very large," agreed the author of *The Country Schoolhouse*.[19] Children's stories certainly bore out such observations; tales of disobedience punished—sometimes mildly, sometimes "very severely"—were legion. In *Parley's Book of Fables*, one story il-

74

lustrated the imprudence of disobedience in the narrative of a little boy who picked a rose against all advice. "Alas, how bitterly did he repent his folly! The stem of the rose was covered with thorns, and his little hand was soon covered with blood." The story showed, Peter Parley told his little friends, "that what may seem very pleasant, may do us harm. . . . Above all, children should never disobey their parents." That little boy got off lightly. In another fable, Parley told of two children who were warned by their parents to stay off the ice on the pond. They disobeyed, fell through the unsafe ice and were drowned.[20]

Even where parents did not directly command, but only recommended, it was dangerous to disregard their wishes. Margaret sulks when her mother says she may not go walking with her new bonnet, her kitten and her dog, because it looks like rain. Mother then decides to let Margaret learn for herself. So Margaret takes bonnet, dog and kitten and goes walking. When the rain comes (as, of course, it does), it is no spring shower, but a terrible storm. Margaret is trapped by a swollen stream, her kitten drowns, the bonnet washes away, and she herself is narrowly saved from watery death by the dog. Needless to say, this experience "entirely cured her of her disobedience."[21]

A corollary virtue to that of obedience, but broader, since it extended beyond parents or other authority, was "submissiveness" or "docility." Submissiveness was that quality in a child which made him put the desires of others ahead of his own. Fictional children were always praised when they subordinated their wishes to those of others. Thus, Emmeline, of *Sarah and Her Cousins*, learned "for the sake of harmony, to give up what she really likes, and to do what was by no means agreeable to her," which the author saw as "highly advantageous to her mind and heart."[22]

Samuel Goodrich, always the least subtle of these authors, gave perhaps the clearest statement of this philosophy in a bald little story called "The Orphans."[23] It is a tale of contrast between an indulged rich boy named Edwin and his cousin Edward, son of a poor but industrious gardener. The two boys play together during the years of their growing up, and Goodrich recounts how their characters develop and diverge as time goes on. Edwin gets everything he wants "because his father was rich," while Edward is "always treated as an inferior" amd "forced to change his plan, if Edwin wished him to do something else."[24] Edward's character improves steadily under this regime; "though he felt that he was sometimes treated with injustice, he still submitted to it without repining."[25] Nothing more happens in the story, and the moral is plainly stated:

> Thus you see that Edwin was now a spoiled child, while Edward was a good, kind and amiable boy. They were both good once, but Edwin had been indulged, and this indulgence had made him passionate, selfish and disagreeable. Edward, on the contrary, by being trained in the habit of giving up his wishes to another, had become even more gentle and generous. Thus you see, my little friends, that indulgence is bad for children, and being made to give up their wishes is good for them.[26]

Submission, or "docility," was especially a necessary ingredient in the reclamation of the wayward characters who were the subjects of so many tales. That wilful girl, Dovey, in *Rollo at School*, is taken in hand by Miss Mary, the schoolteacher, who explains to her earnestly "how much more happily her life would be spent if she would become a gentle, docile, obedient and industrious girl."[27] And there is hope for Dovey precisely because she shows signs of submission. One day Miss Mary watches Dovey and Julius, another inattentive student, as they snap a dry pea back and forth across their desks. She signals them silently to go back to arithmetic—which Dovey does, but which Julius does not, causing Miss Mary to muse to herself: "Dovey gives up at once. That is a good sign. But Julius does not. She yields, he resists. I feel encouraged about her and discouraged about him; for I see in her *submission*, but in him *pertinacity*."[28]

The child who was learning to bend his will to that of his parents, and to put the wants of others above his own, was acquiring that most fundamental component of good character, self-control. And it was precisely *self*-control that was the ultimate object of both obedience and submission. In spite of the theoretical harping on absolute obedience, there was little suggestion in these stories that obedience was simply a matter of authoritarian parents handing down inexplicable commands to puppet-like children. On the contrary, insistence on obedience was nearly always coupled with a strong emphasis on a child's own responsibility for living up to the standards his parents held out to him. Children were expected to internalize, at a very early stage, the principles and precepts of their moral education. Jacob Abbott's Rollo became the standard model of an ideal fictional child at least partly because he so well exemplified the child's role in moral training. Rollo's mother and father were, of course, present in the stories, always issuing appropriate judgments and advice, but they were shadowy figures for all that. It was Rollo's own struggles with his character and conscience through some twenty-eight stories which were most memorable.

Like little Mary, Rollo had a highly-developed conscience at a very tender age. In *The Rollo Philosophy*, he is but five years old, yet well able to undertake sober self-examination if necessary. One chapter of the book tells of Rollo's sulky and ill-natured reaction when a planned blueberrying trip must be called off because of rain. His father, hearing him complain of the weather, speaks to him gravely: "Rollo, did you know you were doing very wrong? You are committing a great many sins, all at once. Your heart is in a very wicked state. You are under the dominion of some of the worst of feelings; you are self-conceited, ungrateful, undutiful, unjust, selfish, and . . . even impious."[29]

Mr. Holiday goes on to explain these charges in detail, dwelling particularly on Rollo's wicked resentment of God's providence in sending a much-needed rain. Rollo then retires to an upper room of the house, especially set aside for the purpose, to meditate. He thinks of what his father has told him and he listens to the rain. From the window, he observes the rain sinking into the ground. "That made him think of the vast amount of good the rain was doing, and he saw his own selfishness in a striking point of view." Acknowledging to himself how wrong he has been, Rollo takes down the Bible and looks into it. There his eyes fall upon the words, "I will arise and go to my father." And Rollo goes to his father to ask forgiveness for his wrong-doing.[30]

In Abbott's stories, as in most others, the expectation was clear: children were to enter into the process of training themselves to achieve principled behavior by examining their performance, their motives, and their hearts. This was known as the "true spirit of obedience," and primarily it required self, not parental, control.

The kind of child nurture recommended by authors of juvenile fiction was entirely consonant with the virtues it was supposed to develop in children. It was rational, rather than authoritarian; kindly, however strict, and designed far more to develop a sensitive conscience in a child than to control through harsh or physical punishment. Severity of standards did not imply severity of method; one story, in fact, attributed the "wild and reckless character" of a boy partly to the errors of the boy's father, "who never gave him any kind and friendly instruction, and always treated him with a great degree of sternness and severity."[31] Children who were "shut up or whipped," according to another author, had their "finer feelings . . . blunted, and their moral nature warped and deformed."[32] Good parents were themselves the best examples of the self-control they wished to inculcate in their children, having long ago learned that "the first step towards ruling others wisely, is to be able to rule one's own self."[33]

In some few instances, physical punishment was recommended—usually for recalcitrant boys who were not the main characters in the story—but the overwhelmingly favored approach to discipline was that of reasoned argument by a calm parent, underscored when necessary by subjecting the erring child to a period of solitary meditation on the evil of his ways. Thus, Herbert, who in anger stepped on his sister's exotic flower, was taken by his mother to his room, "to think on what [he] had done." His mother's sorrow was "more impressive" to him than her anger would have been, and the long day he spent meditating in his room made an indelible impression: "From this time I never again gave vent to my impetuous passions."[34]

Sometimes faith in reason extended to supposing that a child might undertake his own reformation through rational self-examination. Samuel, whose fault of covetousness had alienated all his contemporaries, set about to discover the cause of his unpopularity all by himself. "He . . . confined himself to his room, for some days. There he reasoned with himself on the cause that would produce such treatment from his playfellows. . . . On comparing the good boy's behavior with his own, he very soon discovered the reason." And Samuel reformed, "having learned in what true happiness consists."[35] The "silent system" was considered very likely to be instrumental in personal as well as penal reform.[36]

The major objectives of child training—the self-control, the sensitive conscience, the internalized moral standards—ended, ideally, in a strongly inner-directed character. Nothing so clearly displayed this ideal in operation as the dozens of fictional instances in which a child's effort to live up to the principles he has learned at home met the ridicule of his fellows. The authors recognized the power of ridicule, but they insisted that children could and should stand against it. "It is painful to be laughed at, I confess," one mother told her son, "but you are no longer a mere child, and should have a higher motive of action than the dread of ridicule."[37] Stories held out the assurance that to do right in the face of ridicule would both end the ridicule and "win respect." "Nothing turns the shaft of ridicule so quickly as a frank, bold, manly avowal of right principles. . . . The best way for a boy to avoid ridicule is to prove that he is not afraid of it."[38] There was in this often-repeated theme a tacit recognition of that power of public opinion noted by Tocqueville, Martineau, and other foreign observers of American society, but the authors of children's stories repeatedly urged children to acquire sufficient moral strength to best it.

Yet the influence of public opinion was sometimes not only acknowledged, but brought to bear where it could be useful on the side of right. The consequences of bad behavior were always dire, but varied with the seriousness of the sin. Certain faults, like disobedience or intemperance, if unreformed, led straight to prison or death; but less heinous forms of unacceptable behavior, such as ill temper, procrastination, covetousness or deceitfulness, reaped instead the unhappy harvest of social disapproval. Rosabel Radford, who "never could do anything in a fair and honest manner, but was always planning tricks and trying to decieve [sic]" never reformed, though she was often caught and punished, and at last lost all her friends through her persistent fault. "Everybody was continually watching her lest she should play some trick; and nobody would believe a word she said. All her young friends gave her up, their parents fearing that they would be injured by the example of so bad a girl."[39]

As described in children's stories, the way of even the minor transgressor was hard and lonely, and though he might live out his normal life span—as the seriously wicked rarely did—his passing, when it came, was unmarked and unmourned. Thus, Jane and Louisa, whose differing temperaments formed the basis of the 1828 story, *Happy and Miserable, or, Tempers Contrasted*, furnished useful comparisons in death as in life. "Jane's happy temper continued to bless herself and all about her; and after a long life spent in the exercise of her characteristic virtues, she went to her last home mourned by all who knew her. Louisa, on the contrary, persisted in making herself miserable, and marring, as far as she could, the happiness of others; and died at last without friends, unhonored and unlamented."[40]

Conversely, the fiction often promised social approval to those who kept to the values it taught. Though the idea of virtue for its own sake was a constant in the literature, there was often an additional assurance that one who held staunchly to the ways of right would enjoy the good opinion of others. The child who held out against ridicule "won respect," and so did the young person who asserted his moral responsibility forthrightly, in the face of temptation by others. Cheerfulness was not only an indication of willingness to abide by God's disposing, but was also an attractive trait. Little Mary had to learn to be patiently forbearing because forbearance was a moral virtue, but her mother also suggested that this admirable attitude would insure that her little friends at school would love her.

As the constant emphasis on self-control implied, most literature for children avoided any romantic celebration of untrammeled emotion. The concept of self-control extended to the restraint of almost all displays of strong spontaneous feeling. Authors of children's tales were distrustful of what they called "the passions," which they generally identified with hostile, aggressive, or other antisocial impulses. "Stop, my son!" cried a father to a boy who was killing locusts in anger at what they had done to his fig tree. "That is foolish conduct, and very wicked. You are giving way to anger and revenge, two of the worst passions that a youth can indulge."[41] Wrong feelings were rank weeds that would crowd out the tender shoots of mildness and morality. All the authors knew, as all enlightened fictional parents knew, that "seeds of passion, of self-will, of disobedience and of indolence" had to be "pulled up by the roots" while children were young.[42] Mrs. Child advised children directly: "If you find envy, pride, anger, or vanity growing [in your heart], pluck them up before they have time to injure your character."[43] The human heart was a garden requiring the most careful cultivation.

Control of the passions meant more than simply control over their outer manifestations. It was the feelings themselves which were wrong and which had to be eradicated—"plucked up." Expressions of anger, envy, pride, or any other ugly passion, were taken very seriously in children's fiction—not, certainly, because the authors expected an inborn perfection in children, but because such expressions were indications of wrong feelings which had to be corrected before they grew to unmanageable proportions.

In Abbott's *Caleb in the Country*, an older boy teases a younger one. His grandmother takes him aside to correct him, with that blend of stringent moral reasoning and loving concern so typical of these tales: "What makes me most unhappy," she tells him, "is that my dear Dwight has a heart capable . . . of taking pleasure in the sufferings of a helpless little child." Grandmother acknowledges that the smaller child was not injured in any way by the teasing, but her concern over the incident is, in any case, directed at the inner feelings it has revealed in Dwight's heart: "It is not the mischief that is done, . . . but the *spirit of mind* in you. . . . It is a very little thing, I know; but then it is a little symptom of a very bad disease."[44] Almost exactly the same words are used by the author of *The Daisy* in the case of Johnny, who has given vent to some angry words. His mother has taken him severely to task for his outburst, and Johnny protests that surely "those few words I spoke cannot be *so very* wicked." But his mother replies, "My dear child, a few angry words, or even a fretful look, show the feelings which are in the heart, just as much as a small vane shows which way the mighty winds are blowing." Such things are far from trivial, for the feelings Johnny has revealed show that he is "discontented with [his] own lot. . . . These are the very feelings which lead to dishonest acts in childhood, and to rum-selling, gambling and theft in maturer years. This sinful discontent is the *seed*, and these great crimes are the fruit it bears in the heart."[45] As the *Youth's Companion* observed, "It is one thing to restrain evil dispositions; it is another to have them rooted out."[46] In a society which seemed to be moving away from traditional social restraints while at the same time it embraced a government judged "best when it governed least," it was not enough simply to "restrain evil passions." The awesome freedom of a democracy made personal restraint a perilously frail barrier between society and the antisocial effects of "wrong feelings." Better and safer, the stories said, that evil passions be eradicated altogether—"rooted out"—of the youthful character.

Firm governance of the passions had to proceed, moreover, from the right motives; the most laudable actions were worthless when performed for unworthy reasons. Ellen, one of three little girls being educated by their Mama, inquires during a history lesson about what made "great" such historical figures as Alfred and Alexander and others. Her Mama replies that it is greatness of mind that fits people for the appellation "great," and greatness of mind she defines as supporting misfortunes, forgiving injuries and preferring the good of others to oneself. Ellen concludes that even little girls can do that, and forthwith determines to practice greatness of mind.

Her first triumph comes when her little sister, Lucy, spills ink on the drawing Ellen as been preparing very carefully for a school competition. There is no way for Ellen to repair the drawing, and no time for her to do another, yet she forbears, and shows no anger toward Lucy. "I won't cry, nor yet look cross, though my drawing is quite spoiled, and it is impossible to do another by Thursday."[47]

Mama, when she hears the sad story, commends Ellen: "I congratulate you, my love; you have gained a *conquest* over *yourself* today," and she goes on to point out that "Lucy feels so much gratitude, that she will be very careful not to injure you again in any way." But Ellen is not encouraged to take too much pride too quickly in her new virtue. "Let us examine our MOTIVES before we say we have DONE WELL," suggests Mama. But when Mama and Ellen examine Ellen's motives, they find, alas, that because she was trying to be thought like people "with great minds," Ellen's motive was "as much *pride* as *patience*," and she must try again to achieve an equal level of patience with purer motives.[48] The story goes on to tell of her practising a less adulterated forbearance in a new trial of spirit, and reaping suitable rewards of parental approval.

Goals were set high, and few allowances were made for age or circumstance. A *Juvenile Miscellany* author told a tale of intense school competition, insisting the while that all hard feelings were forbidden: "Emulation is a very good thing, but great care must be taken, that no envy mixes with it." The author considered this feat not only possible, but strengthening: "I know by experience that rivals at school are great trials to a little girl's disposition and temper; but, the only way to be really good, is in overcoming trials."[49] A *Youth's Companion* story told of a good child subjected to a severe trial of conscience when a bad girl killed her pet canary. She successfully put down all feelings of resentment toward the evil-doer, and even proposed to demonstrate to wicked Julia that she has forgiven her. Her aunt counseled against this last, however, lest she should "make the contrast between your conduct and hers too striking . . . there would seem to be an ostentatious display of your forgiveness."[50] Such exacting standards and such closeness of reasoning in their application were the rule rather than the exception in children's fiction.

At least as strongly as they extolled the values of self-denial, the authors of juvenile tales attacked the evils of selfishness. "There is no fault more unpardonable than selfishness, nor any which . . . is more difficult to conquer."[51] The term encompassed every form of preoccupation with self, from "selfish love of ease" to the desire to impose one's will upon others. Even pride in accomplishment came under suspicion, since it might easily descend into conceit, which was an especially virulent form of selfishness, and fatal to any talent: "docility and industry will run over talents clogged with conceit and self-will."[52] No genius, no skill, no cultivated knowledge could balance out the flaw of selfishness; Catherine Sedgwick warned that "selfishness checks the growth of every virtue and casts a shade over every charm."[53]

Like every other form of self-assertiveness, personal ambition was equated with selfishness and was generally disavowed in children's books. In this scrambling, individualistic period of American life, when foreign visitors stepped back in amazement from the vigor of American preoccupation with success, most writers of children's fiction referred to ambition with distaste and distrust. Their ideal children did not have it; their ideal parents did not recommend it. "I don't wish my son to be ambitious;" said an admirable mother of Catherine Sedgwick's creation, "I think it is the fault and folly of our people to be all striving for something beyond them. There is so much said now-a-days about people 'going ahead,' that they are all pushing forward—looking beyond—grasping at something they cannot quite reach, instead of being contented with what they have."[54]

The equation here between ambition and discontent was common to most of the literature and surely reflected a felt reality of a competitive society. Children's stories were full of warnings against restless, footloose behavior and frequent changes of employment; perseverance was far more often praised than enterprise, and contentment with one's given lot was valued over active searching for new fields to conquer. Carlton Bruce's "Story of Tom Restless" purports to tell of a boy who "might have been happy and honored" had he stuck to any one situation, but who "rendered himself miserable by a romantic search after, he did not know what."[55] In fact, the story described—though not very excitingly—a life that seemed more adventurous than miserable, and was a rather attractive contrast with the plodding existence led by most fictional good examples. But Bruce insisted that his message was cautionary: "Never, on slight grounds, relinquish the station in which you are first placed. If you once deviate from the track intended for you, it is no easy matter to recover it."[56] Most authors shared Bruce's uneasiness over young persons who yearned for more than they were born to; Lydia Sigourney offered in praise of education her conviction that "a good education makes us contented with our lot."[57]

Boys were the special targets of much vigorous proselytizing against adventuresome forays into the world far from home. Their books warned against the "insane craving for wealth" that lured young men "to the ends of the earth" or into the "maelstrom of city life."[58] The author of *Harry Winter, The Shipwrecked Sailor Boy* thought his efforts in writing the story would be well spent "if but one lad by reading this brief story, shall be stopt short of his sea-faring notions, and become settled down to his studies, or business; and attentive and dutiful to his parents."[59]

Thus, many authors of children's fiction acknowledged some of the discontents of American life and ascribed them to the restless urging of material ambition. Sensitive to the strain imposed on community and family ties by the generally expansive forces of the period, they opposed the physical and monetary mobility that ambition fostered and questioned the happiness it seemed to promise.

In the credo of children's books, there was in fact small logical place for worldly ambition, since the authors insisted frequently and at length that true happiness was to be found, not in worldly success or material goods, but in a good heart, a good temper and an easy conscience. Catherine Sedgwick's mildly allegorical tale, "The Magic Lamp," illustrated the philosophy generally underwritten by the literature. The heroine of her tale, who met a variety of misfortunes with undaunted spirit, avoided the sin of giving way to grief and despair because she carried with her a "magic lamp." The "magic" of the lamp was in the "oil of cheerfulness" which the heroine herself supplied from her own inner nature. The point of the story was plain: happiness proceeds from

85

within, and has little to do with outer events. The true wellsprings of human content lie in goodness and moral courage.[60] Samuel Goodrich's "Cheerful Cherry" was a somewhat overwrought explication of the same theme, though the resilience of Goodrich's heroine seemed less a product of inner courage than of a remarkable insensitivity to the catastrophes afflicting almost everyone about her. It was central to the message of both stories that happiness was not equated with an absence of trouble. On the contrary, the tales suggested that the kind of happiness that dwelt within a well-regulated human nature was both impervious to the inconsistencies of fortune and a resource for enduring life's inevitable difficulties.

Above all, children were not to believe that material wealth constituted a reliable foundation for happiness, for happiness "does not depend on fine show, nor on bags of silver and gold."[61] Unless they were also virtuous, the wealthy were surely miserable, in spite of their riches. "Be not deceived by the wealth, the popularity, and the glittering gewgaws of the vicious world," advised Uncle Arthur. "If their hearts are not at ease, if their pillow is laid with thorns, all the rest is as nothing: thousands of gold and silver will not lull a guilty conscience to sleep."[62] The authors tried often, and more than a little anxiously, to assure their readers that the success and pleasures of the "vicious" were not real or at least not lasting. Only good is eternal, they reiterated again and again; the "deceitful success" of the wicked soon comes to an end, and the ruthless man however rich, cannot enjoy life.

Instead of the "gewgaws" of material success, authors urged children to understand their goal in life as "usefulness to others." They exhorted young readers to develop their talents and their skills, to be diligent, industrious, persevering and punctual, but never in pursuit of personal success, always in order to "serve others," and to be "useful." They assured them that true happiness was to be found only in selfless service to others, and that misery was the inevitable ultimate consequence of selfishness. The *Juvenile Keepsake* of 1851 carried a story designed to instruct children in "How to Be Happy." In it, Harriet wonders to her mother why she is so much happier today than she was yesterday. "I know I am always happy when I am good," she says, but, though yesterday she was good and had a pleasant day, today she is especially happy. Her mother suggests that she review what she did during the day. Harriet describes a day filled to the brim with entirely altruistic efforts: she has weeded her sister's garden, given away her doll, hemmed a cravat for papa, and so on.

> "Have you done anything for yourself today?" asks her mother.
> "No, Mamma; nothing."
> "Then, now, my love, you can understand. . . . The more useful day has been the happier one. . . . You can never be unhappy while you do everything that is in your power for others, without the hope of recompense. Kindness brings its own reward."[63]

Such sentiments echoed through all the literature. Yet, an attentive child reader might have been excused for expecting more tangible returns for his efforts at moral perfection. For in spite of the many nods in the direction of virtue as its own reward, most children's stories in fact showed moral righteousness repaid by some material success. The bad went down to poverty and death in children's fiction, but the good, after some suffering, to be sure, usually came into the comfort of at least moderate prosperity. Good girls married well; good boys made their way successfully in business.

Dick and His Friend Fidus was an example of this quite typical ambivalence toward the rewards of right doing. Dick, a poor but well brought up boy, faces many trials after he is orphaned, most of them involving moral choices. At every critical juncture, Dick is aided in his perception of the right by the whispered counsel of his friend Fidus—who is, of course, none other than Dick's own carefully nurtured conscience. When Dick follows the dictates of his conscience, things turn out well for him; when he ignores the voice of righteousness, he invariably suffers for it. The ambivalence lies in the nature of the reward and punishment: though the author specifically disavows the connection between right doing and personal advantage, the story belies her claim. In every instance where Dick makes the right moral choice, the consequence involves an improvement in his personal fortune; when he chooses to ignore the advice of Fidus, his rise in the world is interrupted and threatened.

Though this 1859 story was franker in its preoccupation with the material rise of its hero than were most stories of the 1820s, 1830s, and 1840s, the linking of moral virtue and personal prosperity can be found, with varying degrees of subtlety, in much of the children's fiction of the whole period. There were exceptions: Joseph Alden's old Revolutionary soldier, who lived in poverty without the pension to which he was entitled rather than obtain it by means not strictly honest, exhibited the kind of moral scrupulousness highly praised in all the literature. His scruples were well within the code of the fiction, but he was an unusual example of virtue which was indeed allowed to be its own reward. The story did not compensate him in any material way for his acute moral sense, not even with the pension rightfully his. Whatever little comfort he had, had to derive from an easy conscience. While this was theoretically a tenable position, few stories in fact left their characters there. Most authors provided at least a moderately comfortable bed for the sleep of the just.

But even when the authors thus tacitly conceded the desirability of some worldly success, they always implied that such rewards would come automatically to those who practised the moral code endorsed in the books. No hero or heroine was to be seen striving for material advantage, or even taking frank pleasure in material possessions. Children were to concern themselves with virtue and industry; the rest would follow unsolicited. Carlton Bruce's advice to boys to be "industrious, and wise, and virtuous, [that their] young days may be the foundation for the prosperity of manhood, and the comfort of old age" was reflected many times over in the literature. And so was his even plainer promise of the automatic material rewards of virtue: "Self-denial, and industrious application to any honest calling," Bruce told his boy readers, "cannot fail to secure [respectability and influence], and the probability is, that riches will accompany them."[64] With some intensity, children's books implied that the good things of life would accrue to the good in heart through the normal workings of the world, the gratitude of men and the providence of God. If their writing thus betrayed a degree of materialism these writers never consciously admitted, it also indicated, perhaps even more strongly, that the authors wanted to believe that the universe was just and in good moral order, even when the world more immediately around them did not seem to be.

Thus, writers of children's fiction paid tribute to the values of their society without lessening their emphasis on virtue as the foundation of happiness by making economic success and public approval the rewards of moral living. They were sometimes aware of the possibility of confusion in the message: one author tried to distinguish between what she called a "diseased desire of pleasing" and a "laudible [sic] and salutary desire of approbation on account of good actions and virtuous exertions,"[65] but she gave no guidance on how a child might make the distinction in practice. Nevertheless, her position was basically clear, and it was the position of all children's fiction on the matter of virtue and its reward: a desire for the good opinion of others was no fit director for a child's life, any more than was a desire for material gain. Only moral considerations were a proper guide to action, providing as they did the "higher motivation" which was the basis of Christian living. The authors of children's fiction were firm in their insistence that the practice of virtue was to come first. Reward, in the form of prosperity and social approval, would follow of its own accord.

On the whole, authors of children's fiction in this period were quite hopeful about the possibility of molding children into good and moral beings. They by no means underestimated the difficulties—the reality of evil was recognized everywhere in the literature—but they were not pessimistic. Where the eighteenth century, had, theologically at least, viewed child nurture as an uphill struggle against a child's evil tendencies, the nineteenth century was by 1830 moving rapidly toward a more optimistic opinion of human nature, and the fiction for young readers reflected the change, however cautiously.[66]

Most authors avoided an open grappling with the philosophic —or theological—question of whether a child's inborn nature was pure or depraved. If few of these writers clearly abandoned the doctrine of natural depravity (and some of those who wrote for Sunday School publications affirmed it), fewer still took a clear stand in favor of the concept of the child born pure and corrupted thereafter by the world. They endorsed instead a workable, though tacit, compromise between the two positions, most of them describing their major child characters as basically good, but flawed by a fault or two which it was the object of the story to correct. The description of *Self-Willed Susie*, whose behavior becomes quite outrageous at times, is mild, forgiving, and entirely typical: "Save that she was very self-willed, Susie was as good perhaps a little better than the average of children her age."[67] Their position, then, was close to that of Horace Bushnell, whose 1847 treatise on *Christian Nurture* suggested that good and bad potential existed side by side in the inborn nature of a child, and that the duty and point of Christian upbringing was to cultivate the good and control the bad.[68] Fictional children were rarely told by their fictional parents that they were either wholly good or bad. Commentary tended to the specific, dealing with faults to be overcome and virtues to be cultivated or strengthened. And though it was demanding, the tone was generally encouraging. When one little girl lamented that she wished she were "naturally good," her aunt replied without any particular theological precision, "No one is naturally good. . . . To be good, is to love and serve God supremely, and no one does that naturally."[69]

Thus, the ideal child in the earnest literary depictions of the period, unlikely as he seems, maintained at least one important link with reality: he was a being *in process*. He was not a completed product, an infallible creature who never slipped below the high moral standards endorsed in the stories, but an imperfect human personality struggling to become better. Even Jacob Abbott's Rollo, whose preoccupation with moral perfection is so implausibly constant, did not always attain the standards to which he aspired. It was his efforts to live up to them which made him the very image of an ideal child.

For, in that catalogue of qualities expected of a child, that long list which included selflessness, obedience, humility, self-discipline, and the courage to do right in the face of opposition or ridicule, it was the strong and persistent desire to be good that was the central impulse necessary to an ideal child. Everything else hung upon a child's willingness to strive toward the right, to examine his conscience and his motives, and to find satisfaction in the practice of virtue. Even the home nurture which played so central a role in the development of moral character was presented as a kind of dialogue between parent and child, in which the parent was mentor, and the child a willing, searching student of his own moral status.

The goal of the ideal child was to *be good*; the goal of the ideal home was to so train a child as to make goodness possible for him, even in the face of the manifold difficulties the world was sure to present to any human creature. "The early training of a child may be such as to enable him (with the ordinary blessing of God) to pass unscathed through the temptation of the world."[70] Important as it was, home was not pictured in the literature as a haven of safety where a child might linger in security. It was instead a kind of armory which provided a child with weapons against the dangers which lay beyond the doorstep: "Life . . . is ever a conflict," a mother told her son as he prepared to leave home. "The principles which wisdom and truth sanction are not those which govern society."[71] But these words were not said in any attempt to persuade him to stay at home; they were meant to tell him that he must carry within his own heart the principles he had learned at home.

And the child who achieved the ideals of character presented to him by this literature was in truth peculiarly well-adapted to the chancy and threatening reality the fiction so often depicted. The fixed points of his character were internal, rather than external, moral rather than material. His strong inner direction made him psychologically independent at an early age; his moral certainty was a safe guide that carried through every confusion and illuminated the right course of action in every situation, however new, however hostile. An internalized concept of happiness protected him against unpredictable fortune: he could not be brought low by any external disaster, since the center of his content lay within his own heart. Nor could he be demoralized by the opinion of others less enlightened than himself, since the satisfaction of acting from principle was his only acknowledged criterion of success. "Anchored to the rock of principle [and] armed in the panoply of virtue," the ideal child was spiritually free of the dangerous world: "Fortified by the wise counsels of his parents, he felt strong within . . . [and] could mock at the caprices of fortune."[72] He was, in short, safe.

IV

Attitudes and Issues

Books of fiction for children are of their time. However little they may deal directly with social issues, they inevitably convey a good deal about prevailing social attitudes and problems. To be sure, much of what they reveal is outside the conscious intention of their authors; only a few writers of children's fiction in any period treat deeply or even purposely of social questions, and fewer still deliberately engage in matters of controversy. But social attitudes are so much a part of the fabric of life in any era that it is impossible to exclude them from literary efforts. Certainly, a nonfantasy fiction like that written for children between 1820 and 1860 carries considerable evidence in and between its lines about the social views of its authors and some of the realities of their society.

The mood of American society in the second quarter of the nineteenth century was strongly, often stridently, democratic. The celebration of the United States for its equality of condition, its prosperity, and its incomparable opportunities for all people was constant throughout the period and penetrated children's books as it penetrated most popular writing of the time. Authors often remarked upon the egalitarianism of their society, pointing out with pride how America's blessings were open to all: "Unlike other countries, our law and institutions do not favor the rich and great," said Catherine Sedgwick; Americans are "all children of one family."[1] A poor girl who grew up in New England "enjoyed all the privileges of the District and High Schools. In our happy country, the poor as well as the rich may be well-educated."[2]

Children's stories democratically repudiated snobbishness. Fortunate people who looked down on those less wealthy were always described with scorn; it was an axiom of the literature that the only admissible distinction among people was to be based on merit, not money. The girl who stayed aloof from the children of a poor family, "as if fearful of degrading herself by intercourse with those in a humble sphere," was very wrong and in need of a more rational, less fashionable, education.[3] A careful aunt, reprimanding her snobbish niece, who "won't associate with washerwomen" in school, remarked, "God distributes his bounties with an impartial hand . . . yes, there is a difference in rank, but in school, goodness and knowledge should alone determine it."[4] Artificial class distinctions had nothing whatever to do with the truly important differences among people, which were differences in moral behavior. "It is not condition . . . but moral cultivation, which makes us capable of virtuous and disinterested actions. . . . no class is so elevated, as to exclude the operation of mean and unworthy motives."[5]

That snobbishness which attempted to disguise itself as "gentility" drew especially strong criticism from many authors. A young lady in a *Juvenile Miscellany* story offered the opinion that teaching was "not a genteel way of making a living," and received a sharp reply from her friend. " 'Genteel!' said Isabella, impatiently, 'if there is a word in our language, that means any thing and nothing, it is that. I am sure it is a most *un*-genteel word, for it is always in the mouths of the vulgar.' "[6] Catherine M. Sedgwick remarked that the affected gentility of a store clerk's manner "served mainly to attract the underbred."[7]

Certainly there was no room in the pages of this fiction for snobbishness toward any form of honest labor. No honorable employment, the authors assured their young readers, could be degrading; only false pride could lead one to think so. In this view, all children's fiction was united and consistent; there was never the slightest hint that idleness could be preferable to work, or that any work, however menial, was not infinitely more desirable than dependence upon others: "do not . . . consent to live in dependence upon anyone, while you are able to support yourself."[8] This standard advice was given to women and children thrown on their own as often as it was to boys and men. Children's stories supported the dignity of work always, and viewed the fruits of idleness with the deepest distrust.

Such democratic attitudes as these were consciously identified as virtues and took their place in the overall didacticism of the juvenile books. The most fundamentally democratic sentiment advanced in books for children, however, may have been much less consciously assumed than the proclaimed attitudes toward work and snobbishness. The insistence by most of these authors that it was industry and application that accounted for excellence in any field, far more than inborn talent or special intelligence, was truly egalitarian in implication. Like Andrew Jackson, who declared that the work of government could be undertaken by any man of common intelligence, the writers of children's stories taught that any task whatever was within reach of one willing to work at it. Again and again, the stories told children that "industry and attention can accomplish very hard things. . . . There is nothing in which they will not enable you to excel."[9] Even if many children's stories conveyed the impression that it was best not to aspire beyond one's given station in life, and that contentment with one's lot was wiser and safer than ambition, nevertheless, the aspirations of those who chose to ignore this advice were constantly reinforced by the assurances of the fiction that no excellence was beyond the power of hard work to attain. No more democratic a doctrine could have been preached to the children of a society thoroughly imbued with what Bray Hammond has called "the fierce spirit of enterprise".[10] It was ironic that those who so often deplored the restless striving of their time should have so clearly enunciated it.

In fact, though the eager capitalism of the Jacksonian age was not openly embraced by authors of children's books until the 1850s—and then by no means unambiguously—it found expression in the literature in oblique ways throughout the period. A picture of American occupations between 1820 and 1860, for instance, if it were to be assembled from the evidence in children's stories, would be curiously unbalanced and none too accurate, but it would fairly indicate the capitalist spirit of the time.

Farmers were prominent in the literature, as they were in fact, and were frequently held up as models of independent, moral living, but they were present in fiction more to be praised than emulated, apparently—not many central characters in children's fiction were farmers. The professions were nearly invisible. Lawyers were all but nonexistent in stories, and ministers surprisingly rare, considering the religious tone of so much of the writing. Doctors appeared only when called in for consultations; no major adult character was a doctor. Teaching, at least for men, was apparently regarded as an unsatisfactory way to make a living; one story referred to the "irksome life" of a (male) teacher.[11] And, of course, *The Juvenile Miscellany's* vigorous rebuttal of the idea that teaching was "not genteel" suggests that this particular snobbism was not unusual.

Naturally enough, fictional women were very limited in their choice of occupations, as women actually were. If anything, the stories surprise by the number of women they portrayed earning a living—or trying to; it was part of their realism about the perils of poverty to be frank about the difficulties encountered by a woman who had to earn a livelihood.[12] Unmarried women appeared in the books mostly as teachers (and received none of the sympathy extended to male teachers). Married women worked only when driven to it by acute poverty or widowhood (which was often the same thing); they were then seamstresses or, in the most abject cases, laundresses or domestic help. Factory work for women was almost never acknowledged in children's stories, though after 1830 it was, in reality, increasingly the resort of women who had to support themselves.[13] Fictional counterparts of many of the authors, that is, women who made a living by writing, rarely appeared in their stories.[14]

The most visible occupations were those connected with business. Far and away the most favored occupation for a fictional father, especially if he was financially successful, as most ideal fathers were, was that of merchant. The father of a main character usually paid his respects to the satisfactions of the agricultural life, praising its independence and morality, and he often took his children for instructive trips to the country, pointing out the beauties of nature and discoursing learnedly on botany and natural history. He might even, in a moral or physical crisis, send his children to country relatives for rehabilitation, but he himself, if he was a man of comfortable income, usually earned his living in commerce.

Those fictional boys who chose their life work in the course of the stories followed the same pattern. They rarely became farmers or went to college or entered the professions. They went instead into business, usually in some merchant house or shop, presumably to work their way up through the ranks. Jacob Abbott's engaging character, Beechnut, who came into his legacy at seventeen and had to choose how best to use it in launching himself on a career, provided a variation, but only a small one. Abbott gave the whole of Beechnut's logic in making the decision not to use his money for higher education: "If I go to college, I shall expend all my money and have nothing to begin the world with. If then, when I had got through, I should fail in getting into business in my profession—and a great many do fail—I should lose all I have, and be nothing at all. It is too great a risk for me to run." So Beechnut took the unusual (for these stories) step of going into ship carpentering as a trade. But he did so because he had capital with which to build his own business when he had learned his trade, and Abbott ended his tale with a brief sketch of Beechnut's very rapid rise in the business he had so logically chosen.[15]

In such ways, children's fiction gave evidence, both direct and indirect, that the authors accepted many of the social and economic values of their society. Nevertheless, as the stories also indicated, the acceptance was never wholesale, never unequivocal. Writers frequently revealed a vague but broad-gauged uneasiness about their own time, most characteristically expressed in their tendency to idealize the recent American past. Their celebration of the yeoman farmer at a time when it was already apparent that his pattern of life belonged more to the past than to the future was a case in point. Even more pervasive were the dozens of small asides and fleeting remarks by which juvenile stories implied that the past was better and purer, higher minded and freer of the corruption of greed than was the present. Admiration for the past appeared most often as an admiration for the moral character of an earlier generation; men and women of the earlier time were

97

"stronger" and "better" than contemporary people. George Washington was always the foremost example of the higher standards of character which had prevailed among Americans of his time, and children's fiction usually suggested that if Washington's childhood virtues could but be instilled in this rising generation, the American future would be as glorious as the American past. The sense that the moral tone of American society had declined since Washington's day was a strong undercurrent running through much of the literature.[16]

Some ambivalence also lay beneath the avowedly democratic social values espoused in children's books. Broadly speaking, the social attitudes set out in the stories were those of democratic middle-class society, which disapproved snobbishness and fashionableness, yet retained a rather patronizing, though kindly, attitude toward the poor. In spite of their steady repudiation of snobbishness, children's fiction often indicated that the authors were sensitive to class differences. No doubt they were sincere in their endorsement of the equality of American institutions, and no doubt their dislike for the crass snobbery that made honest labor an object of contempt was real enough. All the same, many writers did not altogether conceal a patronizing attitude toward those they called "the humble," nor hide their feeling that aspiration was somehow connected with station.

Station, with attendant notions of appropriate behavior, aspiration and even dress, was a concept still very much alive in many of the books. No one was supposed to concern himself with any kind of "show" in dress or possessions; certainly it did not do for a girl of limited means to feel proud, or to want to "appear smarter [more rich] than, situated as she is, she ought to appear."[17] It was neither wise nor truly charitable in those who were helping the poor to put exalted notions into their heads. Charles Bolton, who has brought a worthy orphan, Tommy, to his father's attention, is pleased to hear that Mr. Bolton plans to buy Tommy some new clothes, and he remarks to his mother that now Tommy will "look like somebody." Whereupon Mrs. Bolton quickly replies, "That is not in the least necessary, or to put one idea in his head that might tend to make him forget his station in life, or feel dissatisfied with that condition in which God has been pleased to place him; to do so would be doing him a serious injury." Tommy is to be put on his way to earning a decent and honest living, but he is not to look toward an occupation beyond his "station in life." And so it turns out: when Charles goes to see him fifteen years later, he finds him working in a grocery shop, still showing "the same respectful manner he had ever shown as a boy," which shows, the author concluded, "how much depends upon a child's character and deportment."[18]

Of course, any child's character and deportment were important, but the child in a "humble station" needed a certain sense of fitness about his own place in order to be pleasing. The same author who thought that moral behavior had nothing to do with class furnished a remarkably blunt statement of the qualities that made a poor girl attractive to the wealthier family which had taken her in: "There was a feeling of inferiority on her part, which, operating together with kind treatment, on a gentle and affectionate temper, rendered her not only humble and grateful, but disinterested and devoted. It is this which renders her so pleasing."[19]

Some stories written to encourage the charitable impulse seemed to assume that the poor had no tastes of their own, no life that could not be perfectly well manipulated and probably improved by charitably-inclined betters. Eliza Leslie told a Christmas story which was doubtless meant to suggest how much better it was to give than to receive. She established the worthiness of the poor boy who is to do the receiving when her heroine said, "His mother must be a nice woman, for though their income is very small, Edwin always makes a genteel appearance, and is uniformly clean and neat."[20] Edwin's genteel appearance qualified him for the charitable attentions of Amelia and Oswald, daughter and son of a well-to-do businessman, and, in due time, of their father as well. Mr. Woodley, in fact, was so struck by Edwin's honesty and respectful manner, that he invited him to join the Woodley family at Christmas dinner. No one reflected that Edwin's family (he had one) might want him home for Christmas Day—not even Edwin, who "arrived, looking very happy." The Woodley family "were all delighted with his modesty and good sense," and Mr. Woodley continued to act as benefactor to the whole of Edwin's family, so that they were "enabled to occupy a better house, and to live once more in the enjoyment of every comfort."[21]

Even Catherine Maria Sedgwick, who was certainly a more thorough-going democrat than Miss Leslie, felt free to suggest to an Irish laborer that he could well do without his drink with "the boys" in order to send his children to school. "Surely, surely, Mr. O'Neil," said the model heroine of Mill-Hill, "those that have children to play with when they come in from their work don't need a drink to cheer them!"—to which Mike O'Neil obligingly and respectfully replied, "And that's true, Miss."[22]

Stories which imputed to the poor a becoming gratitude and respect toward those who have shown them kindness were very numerous, and plainly were designed to make the duty of charity attractive to those of means. In their efforts to promote charity, however, some authors seemed to overlook more fundamental solutions to economic inequality. "The Mysterious Benefactor," by Miss Edgarton,[23] was one of those curiously purblind tales, increasingly common in the 1850s, which looked straight at a social problem and declined to see it. It told of Fanny and her widowed mother, who barely eked out a living sewing for a local merchant. They were befriended and seen through the mother's serious illness by Cassie, a young lady who posed as a milliner's daughter, but who was actually the daughter of the merchant for whom they worked. When they discovered her real identity, they were intensely grateful for her charity, but Fanny felt "not so free" with Cassie as when she thought her a milliner's daughter. At no time did it occur to any of the characters that Cassie's charity and Fanny's gratitude would have been less needful if the merchant had paid better wages.

Other authors, just as wedded to the concept of private benevolence as the right response to poverty and need, were less sentimental about the uses of charity. Many let their readers know that the best form of charity was not simple bounty, but that assistance which helped the poor to become independent. It was the truest charity "to put people in the way of helping themselves," according to Laura's aunt in *Laura's Impulses:* "It is easy to give, but in relieving the present want, we may really injure the character and habits of the person, if he thus becomes willing to depend on others."[24]

The philosophy of Charles' mother, in *The Way to Do Good,* [25] was the same. Charles asks his mother if he may give an old pair of his shoes to a poor boy who has none. "Well, my dear," replies his mother, "I do not think you should give him your shoes, for I am not sure that it would be a good thing for him; it might make him idle, and like to beg rather than to work . . . you would, perhaps, be doing him harm, instead of good." She suggests instead that "our man, John," be asked if he needs some help in the garden, so that the boy may work for the money with which to buy shoes. "But how can he work in the garden without shoes?" asks Charles. To which his mother replies, "I do not think it will hurt his feet a bit more to work in the garden than to walk in the road, Charles, and if we can teach this boy to work for what he wants, instead of begging for it, we should do him much more good than if we were to give him ten pairs of shoes."[26]

This practical attitude was often coupled with the equally practical advice that an expectation of gratitude was no part of a reasonable approach to charity. Laura, who had offered to teach some poor Irish children to read, was soon bored with the task and chafed at their lack of gratitude, causing the author to remark, "Ah, Laura did not know that when we begin to open a debt and credit account of the benefits we confer and the appreciation we expect on the other side, it will not lighten our efforts."[27] Right was to be done "because it was right, not because you want anybody to pay you, or thank you, or praise you for it."[28] In this view, at once realistic and idealistic, charity was the duty of those who could afford it, to be undertaken for its own sake, and managed so as to do the maximum good. Properly administered, charity promoted reform and improvement amongst the poor. According to Catherine Sedgwick, "it is a help and incentive to amendment to the most degraded to feel that they are cared for by the good and respected."[29]

The discussions of station and of charity offered abundant evidence that consciousness of class differences had by no means disappeared under the democratic waves. References to "the humble" were sometimes insensitive, sometimes decidedly colored by a sense of superiority. Yet there was broad acceptance of the fluidity of social class in most of the literature; one reason manners were so important was because class lines were so flexible. As Mrs. Child pointed out in the preface to *The Little Girl's Own Book*, "In this country it is peculiarly necessary that daughters should be so educated as to enable them to fulfil the duties of a humble station, or to dignify and adorn the highest."[30] The child born in a cottage might well end in a mansion. And, in spite of some condescension, the prevailing tone of the literature toward the poor or lower-class citizen was neither harsh nor unfeeling. On the contrary, most stories displayed a genuine compassion toward the unfortunate.

Perhaps the best example was the attitude in the fiction toward the Irish. Many of the Irish who came to the United States in these years were truly oppressed; their poverty seemed more dire and more stubborn, their ignorance and their needs more staggering, than those of most poor Americans. A description in *The Morton Family* of an Irish household was as restrained as most description in this fiction, yet it conveyed something of the horror many Americans felt at their first glimpse of Irish poverty:

> Mrs. Morton went with her children to the abode of the Irish emigrants, and there they witnessed a scene of misery which almost baffles the powers of description. The family consisted of Mr. and Mrs. O'Connor and ten children; some straw, spread in one corner of the apartment, constituted their only bed; on a broken table lay the remains of their last repast; their clothes afforded but a slight protection from the inclemency of the weather, and they had no means of procuring food for the next day, except from imploring charity.[31]

A *Juvenile Miscellany* story used almost the same language to describe the terrible poverty of an Irish family in New York. How unaccustomed an American child was to such a sight was suggested by the reaction of the little girl who had accompanied her mother there on a charitable visit. She "looked around, and burst into tears."[32]

In addition to their poverty, the Irish had other liabilities from the point of view of many Americans. Their ways were foreign and their religion Papist; they were unlettered, unskilled, and often unruly. Most disturbing of all, perhaps, the immigrant Irishman of the period represented a new and most unwelcome social problem for the rapidly industrializing United States: he was the symbol of a new class of urban, industrial poor.

To this troublesome presence, many Americans of older stock reacted with hostility; anti-Catholic and anti-Irish feeling was common in the Jacksonian age. The description by Catherine Sedgwick of the reactions of ordinary American citizens to the Irish may be taken as typical: "When the new railroad that runs near Mill-Hill was to be made, the neighborhood was alarmed. They dreaded the Irish, whom they regarded as savages." Miss Sedgwick, however, made it clear that she did not share this prejudiced reaction. "I do not think we shall have any trouble from them if we only treat them right," said her heroine, Emma, and the remainder of the tale told of Emma's steadfast and successful efforts to extend the help of the "good and respected" to these immigrants, as to all others in need of charity and guidance.[33] The lower social position of the Irish in the story could scarcely be doubted, but Emma's charity toward them was unfailing, if somewhat managing.

Catherine Sedgwick was not unusual in the kindliness of her attitude toward the Irish; it was the standard in children's fiction. Though the place of the Irish in American society of the period was accurately indicated in the stories—they were laborers or servants—and they were sometimes set apart by their speech, occasionally by their "comic" possibilities,[34] there was seldom real hostility in these characterizations. References to the troubles that brought the Irish to America were sympathetic and some authors defended them against charges of idleness. The most frequent description of the Irish was "warm-hearted."[35]

There were exceptions: Aunt Julia's *The Temperance Boys*

described the drunken, shiftless parents of some destitute children, who would not work when work was available, and who accepted charity, even signed the pledge and went on drinking. The author refrained from calling these immoral creatures Irish, but their speech ("The houly Virgin bless ye!") sufficiently identified them.[36] In general, however, the anti-Irish sentiment of the period was most discernible in the authors' efforts to counter it with Christian charity.

In addition to a democratic zeal, the years before the Civil War were marked by a passion for reform. "What a fertility of projects for the salvation of the world!" Emerson exclaimed. Certainly not all the mutifarious reform movements of the mid-nineteenth century found expression in children's fiction. Of Emerson's litany of movements, "of homeopathy, of hydropathy, of mesmerism, of phrenology."[37] children's stories had little to say. Nor did the devotees of vegetarianism, unleavened bread, multiple marriage, or free love advertise their solutions to the world's ills in this literature. Most of those who wrote for children gave their first allegiance to the settled values of home, family, and the established institutions of society, seeking more often to salvage the virtues of the past than to turn society upside down in order to improve the future.

Yet the values cherished by most of these authors could and sometimes did lead straight into the heart of some of the widest reform movements of the time. If war and drink and slavery were destroyers of home, family, and the order of society, then antiwar, antislavery, and temperance were reform efforts congenial to the thinking of many authors of children's literature. A good many of the authors did, in fact, follow the logic of their values into the ranks of these movements, and they sometimes incorporated their special reform messages into the broader moral didacticism of their juvenile stories.

Antiwar sentiment was fairly common in children's fiction throughout the period, reflecting the peace movement that ebbed and flowed in the United States between the War of 1812 and the Civil War. Pacifism drew its greatest support from New England and the free states of the northeastern seaboard, where most authors of children's books lived, and had close ties in the 1830s and 1840s with the antislavery movement, with which many of the authors also sympathized.[38] The peace argument in juvenile fiction generally turned upon Christian principle and social progress—never upon the acute political problems that underlay the movement. Authors of children's literature dealt, as usual, in universals. Hate and killing in war were against God's law, and were socially retrogressive. Antiwar authors pointed out that war "retards the progress of religion, civilization, and morality. It fosters the worst passions of human nature."[39] They described war as a "savage and brutalizing occupation, disgraceful to a civilized and enlightened age . . . the resort of restless and ambitious men . . . [and] the cause of great suffering." Characteristically for this literature, the anti-war writers understood the causes of war in personal terms. Ruthless men—rulers and generals, monarchs and government ministers—made wars; they "hold the happiness of their species cheap."[40] Sometimes economic motives were blamed; merchants who saw the possibility of rich profits "affect[ed] patriotism" to promote war, according to one author.[41]

The story of *Charles Ashton, The Boy That Would Be a Soldier*, employed most of the standard antiwar arguments of the period, together with the accepted techniques for indoctrinating the young. Charles' father is a minister who opposes war. When his son expresses a desire to become a soldier, Mr. Ashton says that he will not dictate but will educate his son on his choice of profession. This he proceeds to do by means of rational discussion, considerably aided by the personal reminiscences of an old soldier and a disillusioned colonel of the army.

The old soldier furnishes the ever-useful bad example. He is a drunkard, corrupted by his exposure to the wickedness of the ordinary soldier's life, which is filled with gambling, drinking, and foul language. Soon after Charles has made his acquaintance, the old soldier, who has tried without success to reform his evil habits, dies in a drunken stupor. Charles is horrified by the manner of his death, but his father points out how much worse it is for those soldiers who die in battle, swearing and full of hate, trying to kill their fellow men.

Then Charles is taken by his father to meet the Colonel, who

105

relates to the boy some very graphic descriptions of the horrors of war, including the burning of Moscow and the terrible retreat of Napoleon's army from Russia.

> No language can describe the horrors of this scene. . . . The roads and plains were covered with the wretched inhabitants. . . . Robbery, murder, outrage of every sort marked their path . . . neither age, rank, or sex were spared. Cold and hunger rapidly destroyed the ill-fated soldiers. . . . Badly clothed, badly mounted, without food, without drink, groaning with pain . . . [they] laid themselves down to die in the snow, which speedily covered them, and served for their graves.[42]

And who gained? the Colonel asks at the end of his recital. "Who was happier, who was richer, who more contented, who more free? . . . It was a fruitless, profitless war."[43]

Joseph Alden's *Old Revolutionary Soldier* was equally graphic about the brutalities of war and, more surprising, he tied his theme to the behavior of American soldiers during the Revolutionary War. Service in an army, even the Revolutionary Army, was anything but romantic in his description. Discomfort and impiety dominated his account, but real cruelty was not missing. He told of American soldiers plundering their own people, eating the food of a starving, sick woman, and striking the child who tried to prevent them. The soldiers justified their behavior, the old soldier said scornfully, "by calling the people Tories."[44]

Usually the American Revolution was exempt from the strongest strictures of the antiwar writers, since the Revolution was regarded as "a just cause," and "a good man may . . . fight in a just cause." George Washington, who was praised as the highest example of a good man, was also—and this was invariable—"an exception to all great soldiers" in the high morality of his character and motives.[45] Even Alden, strictest of all the pacifists, allowed that the Revolution was "the most just war ever entered into on political grounds."[46]

All the same, Alden's old soldier did not soften facts for his patriotic young listener. "There are very few cases in which it is right for a man to be a soldier," he told Ezra, and when Ezra said that he thought the Revolution was a fight for just rights and that the Lord was in favor of it, the old soldier agreed, but only with reservations. "It will do you good to know the truth," said the old man. Good men did take part in the Revolution, and probably God meant for America to resist Britain, but "a camp is a camp, and . . . it is a place where of all places sin flourishes the most."[47] Charles Ashton's father also conceded the justice of the Revolutionary cause, but in the next breath told his son that, in *most* cases, nothing on either side justified recourse to war, and pointed out that if his son became a soldier, he would have no choice about whether he would fight or not, however he judged the justice of the cause.

In every effort at antiwar education, the authors saw their first task as that of stripping war of its supposed glory. While children were brought up to believe that war is "glorious or a necessary or even useful custom, there can be no hope for peace," explained the author of *Charles Ashton*.[48] In presenting strongly realistic accounts of war's death and devastation, antiwar advocates hoped to overcome the popular tendency to glorify military heroism by showing, as vividly as possible, the horror and futility of war. Little children got capsule descriptions, but strong ones: "Oh, what sad sights are to be seen where a battle has been fought! The poor soldiers lie scattered over the field, some of them already dead, and some of them dying, . . . the grass is stained with blood."[49] Older children were offered even sterner fare, like Lydia Sigourney's "Frank Ludlow," a sentimental but grim story of a young soldier shot for desertion.[50]

There was in fact little glorification of war in children's books of the period; the aggressive instincts were as little admired on the national as on the personal level. If only a few stories carried a specifically antiwar message, fewer still dramatized war in exciting tales of heroism and danger. The Revolution was referred to, fleetingly and usually admiringly, and so was George Washington, whose irreproachable character and reputation for obedience to his mother particularly sanctified him in the eyes of these writers, but the obvious opportunities to make use of the Revolution for thrilling stories were generally bypassed. Exciting tales of military heroism, brilliant uniforms, trumpets and drums—all took their place in the long rolls of temptations to be resisted: " 'The drum and fife, Harry! . . . Don't you hear them?' 'Yes, I hear them, and can resist them, too,' said Harry proudly."[51] So did most authors of juvenile fiction before 1860.

Of all reform efforts, temperance probably generated the largest quantity of writing aimed specifically at children. An attempt to proselytize children early on the subject followed logically from the general persuasion of the time about the importance of early training, as well as from the temperance reformer's special faith in the pledge of total abstinence as effective innoculation against the evils of alcohol. Though a great deal of temperance propaganda for children, as for adults, was nonfictional, some of it was embedded—none too deeply—in stories, since writers considered fiction an effective way to catch and keep the attention of their young audience. Besides, the dramatic notions held by temperance workers about the plummeting descent of a drinker from first drink to total dissipation furnished a strong, ready-made story line which was easily garnished with dramatic details and, of course, suitable lessons.

Temperance propaganda, whether for adults or for children, tended to be heavy-handed. The goal was total abstinence, and in pursuit of that end, the literature dwelt as vividly as possible on the dangers of drink. All the usual literary devices of children's fiction were employed to carry the message. There were rational discussions between parents and children, visits to the poverty-stricken homes of drunkards, tales of contrast between the fortunes of those who took to drink and those who vowed early to abstain, and, of course, countless variations on the awful and instructive example, whose suffering degradation and—usually —death was exhibited as the inevitable result of drinking.

Moderation was no part of the temperance vocabulary. Those who fought the battle against alcohol were deeply persuaded of its power to enslave; they were sure that one drink could, and a daily drink surely would, produce a hopeless craving for liquor.

After 1836, the temperance movement formally embraced total abstinence as its goal, believing, as an 1859 tale explained, that "most of those who start, never find the right place for stopping."[52]

Even the briefest tale for the youngest child was likely to compress this philosophy into the kind of capsule horror story that became a cliche of the movement:

> There was once a little boy who used to drink the sugar left in the tumbler where his father had taken his morning dram. He soon began to like not only the sugar, but the fiery rum mixed with it, and went on gradually from one degree to another, till he became a moderate drinker, then a habitual drunkard, and finally died of delirium tremens. Observe his progress . . . to a drunkard's grave.[53]

Both plot and thesis were elaborated for older children. The magnitude of the problem was stressed: "Ardent spirit is a poison. It kills 30,000 people in this country every year."[54] And the terrible effects of the drunkard's weakness on those who depended upon him were detailed in innumerable tales; the squalor of a drinker's home, the misery of his destitute family, the suffering of wife or child physically abused by a father crazed with drink were all staples of the temperance tale. Some stories even showed the sad plight of children cursed with a drunken mother.

The Brandy Drops, by Aunt Julia, was a model temperance story for children. "The best way is for people to promise while young never to drink, and then they will not learn to love it," says a father to his two sons. Persuaded by their parent's rational arguments, the boys decide to take the pledge, but before they succeed, they meet some of the tests of moral courage so regularly encountered in the literature. They are ridiculed by the other boys at school for their intention. Charlie, especially, is daunted by the jeering, and worse, is tempted into ill humor. "It was very unwise in him to do so [express his annoyance], for many of the boys would have taken his part if he had shown a little more lovable temper about it. . . . It is very poor policy to be ill-natured."[55]

At school the following day, Charlie denies that he means to take the pledge. The boys then tempt him into eating a good many brandy drops [candy], which make him feel very queer; in fact, they evidently make him drunk. The next thing he knows, he is at home in his own bed, his grieved parents watching over him. He confesses all, and begs their forgiveness. His parents do, of course, forgive him, pointing out at the same time all the useful lessons to be learned from his experience. Besides an appreciation for the ill-effects of alcohol on the human frame, Charlie has learned that his parents' advice is to be preferred over that of his peers, that his fear of ridicule was his chief undoing, and that it is wiser to flee than to stay where temptation lures.

In addition to arguing for vows of total abstinence, many temperance tales also tried to persuade people to boycott those who sold alcoholic liquors. According to the temperance code, the sellers of ardent spirits entered into the sin of the drinkers, sharing the responsibility for the dereliction alcohol caused. Moreover, anyone who traded with a seller of liquor, even if he bought only groceries of him, became in turn "a partaker in his evil deeds, and a sharer in the profit of his abominable traffic."[56]

Temperance writers apparently encountered a class resistance from some who were willing to concede that temperance vows and temperance societies were devices useful enough for the lower levels of society, but unnecessary for those of better class. One of Aunt Julia's tracts included a substory in which a Mr. Williams admitted that temperance societies were all very well for the "lower classes," but "not necessary for intelligent persons." His visitor, a most respectable gentleman and keenly "temperance," replied that on the contrary, respectable people "must set the example," or the lower classes will not join temperance societies: "The very reason we have so many drunken foreigners here, Irish, English, German, etc., is because they have not been taught total abstinence at home by respectable people."[57] *Well Enough for the Vulgar* attacked the same problem. In this tale, "Fashionable" people who scorned temperance as fit only for servants and other poor folk, met their just fate when their son, whom they had taught to drink, become a hopeless drunkard.[58]

Temperance was very much the kind of reform cause which

could be widely and safely endorsed in children's fiction. It was not controversial; the problem was real and wide-spread, and there were few who would have argued against efforts to warn children away from the evils of immoderate drinking. Indeed, the general acceptance of the temperance message was sufficiently demonstrated by its constant presence in the *Youth's Companion*. That cautious journal, which explicitly excluded controversial material from its pages, published hundreds of temperance tales during the period.

And warnings against the dangers of drink were not confined to specifically temperance tracts. Many authors who never allied themselves formally with the movement, and who did not concern themselves or their stories with pledges or temperance societies, spoke out in a general way against the evils of alcohol and the inevitable price of drunkenness. In fact, so commonplace was the antiliquor sentiment in children's stories that it was often scarcely identifiable as a reform crusade. To inveigh against the danger of drink and to warn children of the fate of the drunkard was nearly as standard in the literature as to admonish them against the perils of disobedience.

The antislavery cause, on the other hand, was highly controversial, especially after 1831, the year of the Nat Turner rebellion, the first debate on slavery in the Virginia legislature and the opening salvos of Garrison's *Liberator*. The appearance of antislavery sentiment in children's fiction was, accordingly, relatively rare in the general book trade; certainly, compared to temperance, the antislavery cause received sparse treatment. Not surprisingly, some of the strongest antislavery stories for children were published by special presses—The American Reform Tract and Book Society, and the Juvenile Emancipation Society, for instance—most of them in the late 1840s and 1850s. That antislavery sentiment which did enter the mainstream of juvenile literature was not only unusual, but, with rare exceptions, it was muted and indirect.

Two popular writers of children's fiction were active workers in the crusade against slavery. Eliza Lee Follen and Lydia Maria Child were both members of several antislavery societies, in-

111

cluding the American Anti-Slavery Society after its formation in 1833. Both wrote extensively on behalf of the cause, and both incorporated antislavery views into some of their writing for children. With one exception, in a story by Mrs. Child, both authors handled the issue of slavery with caution and restraint.

Eliza Follen, born Eliza Lee Cabot in Boston in 1787, well-educated and well-connected, wrote and edited in the field of juvenile literature from the 1820s through the 1850s. Most of her writing was aimed at the Sunday School libraries; much of the fiction was little more than a vehicle for religious or general educational instruction. Her first full-length book for children, *The Well-Spent Hour*, published in 1827, was a conventional tale, thoroughly laced with instruction—religious, moral, and scientific—and containing no mention of slavery. The book was very popular—it was in its third edition five years later, when Mrs. Follen followed up that success with *A Sequel to the Well-Spent Hour, or The Birthday*. In this ordinary moral-by-contrast tale of two girl cousins, the author's antislavery views made a brief, rather tentative appearance. Mrs. Nelson, mother of the model cousin, told the two girls about a Negro woman who lived for seven years in the North Carolina woods with her two young sons in order to remain near her husband, still in slavery nearby. Such a deed should stand as an example, Mrs. Nelson said, to all those "who had ever failed to do honor to the immortal nature of the Negro."[59] While the anecdote certainly had some import in 1832, when the climate of opinion over slavery was increasingly stormy, it was only an aside in the main narrative of this tale. There were no further comments on its meaning; the author undertook no condemnation of slavery as an institution.

Mrs. Follen again revealed her sympathy for the Negro in one of her 1858 *Twilight Tales*, though she again avoided clearly abolitionist statements. "May Mornings" described a May festival held in the District of Columbia to which all children, rich and poor, were invited—except slave children: "But there are many poor children who are never invited . . . they are slaves—they are negroes."[60] These remarks were followed by the sentimental story of Harry, a little Negro boy, very good and kind, who was rudely treated by one of a group of while children, a big boy who called him "nigger" and "darky." The other children rallied to Harry's aid, and Harry himself soon "returned good for evil," thus converting the erring boy to a more humane view of color differences.[61] Whether or not Harry was a slave child was not clear from the story; Mrs. Follen's concern here seems to have been with color prejudice. Abolition of slavery was not mentioned in either anecdote; Mrs. Follen only advised her young readers not to forget the slave: "When you are men and women . . . you may do much for the poor slaves. Remember them then, and do not forget them now. All can do something for them, even little children."[62] But what they were to do, as children or as adults, Mrs. Follen did not say.

Lydia Maria Child declared her views more openly, if only occasionally, in her writing for children. *Evenings in New England*, published in 1824, included the earliest expression for children of her views on slavery. Much of the story is in the form of a dialogue between two children, Lucy and Robert, and their learned and rational aunt. Robert opens the discussion on slavery by suggesting that Southern people must be "very cruel" to keep slaves. That opinion is unjust, his aunt replies, for, though slavery is a "stain," yet for Southerners it is "their misfortune more than their fault." Their best men would gladly be rid of it, and sometime will be. Slavery is an inheritance from colonial days; when Americans of that time petitioned the British government to have it removed, they were refused. Now it is a "fixed habit," and difficult to remove. Also, Negroes are now numerous and unused to liberty. If they were freed suddenly, they would become licentious and abandoned. Consequently, aunt concludes, good men must follow a reasoned course of action, first, to make slaves as comfortable as possible; second, to instruct their children; third, to give freedom to those who deserve it; and finally, to use their influence to end slavery. "Our Southern brethren," says the aunt, "have an abundance of kind and generous feeling . . . [yet] the system of slavery no doubt makes many of them proud, indolent and tyrannical." Thus instructed, Robert decides that if he had a little slave, he would teach him to read and write and then "send him to Hayti," where he would be "as free and happy as I am."[63]

Mrs. Child's 1824 position was broadly acceptable doctrine in the north at that time. It carefully separated the slaveholder from the "system of slavery," avoiding moral judgment on the master while condemning the institution and assigning basic responsibility for slavery to British colonial rulers. It was at most a very gradualist proposal for change. Though the institution was deplored, the number of slaves and their poor preparation for freedom were cited as reasons for leaving the system in force while long-range solutions were underway. Robert's suggestion that he would send a freed slave to Hayti paralleled the basic concept of the American Colonization Society, of which Mrs. Child was a member before Garrison's attack on its theory convinced her that the plan was unworkable.

From 1826 to 1834, Mrs. Child edited *The Juvenile Miscellany*, a bimonthly publication for children offering both fiction and nonfiction, much of which she wrote herself.[64] Though her commitment to abolition deepened over this period, and especially between 1830 and 1833,[65] she by no means turned the *Miscellany* into a forum for her antislavery opinions. References to slavery were few, and often both brief and gentle. Little children were urged to love one another regardless of color, because "God made the little black children to differ from the white ones."[66] Nonfictional articles might make the point by analogy, as did a comment on slavery in Brazil: "The worst of all evils in Brazil is slavery; indeed it is the greatest evil that can exist in any country. It is sure to bring misery upon those who encourage it, as well as upon those who suffer by it."[67] But direct assaults upon American slavery were rare.

Just once, in 1830, Mrs. Child wrote a clear and ringing condemnation of slavery for *The Juvenile Miscellany*, and she chose a fictional framework to carry it. "Jumbo and Zairee" is the tale of two young Africans, brother and sister, who are captured by slave traders and taken by American slave ship to Georgia. There they are purchased by a kind and decent master, who treats them well—but a footnote to the story here remarks that "this is generally the case with slaves at the south; but the *principle* is wrong, even if there are nine hundred and 99 good masters out of a thousand."[68] In spite of their good master, Jumbo and Zairee, in time, encounter some of the cruelties of slavery. Zairee is whipped by command of a wicked overseer. In anguish at seeing her hurt, Jumbo tries to kill the overseer, and for this rebellion, is sold twenty miles away. Zairee is so grieved by separation from her brother that she cannot eat, which alarms the overseer. He forces her to eat by threatening her with more whipping.

It was at this point in her story that Mrs. Child interjected a passionate outcry against the system which allowed such treatmen to human beings: "This was in the United States of America which boasts of being the only true republic in the world! the asylum of the distressed! the only land of perfect freedom and equality! Shame on my country—everlasting shame! History blushes as she writes the page of American slavery, and Europe points her finger in derision."[69] Not even the reform press juvenile stories spoke out so strongly on slavery as a national disgrace and a clear violation of the principles of American democracy.

The story is resolved when Jumbo and Zairee, together with their father, who has turned up by remarkable coincidence, are all three bought and returned to Africa by a slaveholder who has become convinced of the wrongness of slavery. "I have tried to show my gratitude to the Negroes by being a kind master," this gentleman says, "but I am satisfied this is not all I ought to do. They ought to be free."[70] In 1830, it was still the hope of most of those opposed to slavery that slaveholders could be brought by moral suasion to just such a view of their duty toward the Negro.

The story of Jumbo and Zairee was by far Mrs. Child's most outspoken indictment of slavery in her writing for children. Interestingly, it seems not to have had any very strong immediate repercussions. Though it was published in 1830, *The Juvenile Miscellany* continued to thrive, and Mrs. Child continued to be a very popular and successful writer for both adults and children. It was only after 1833, possibly as a result of the publication of her powerful antislavery essay for the general public, *An Appeal in Favor of That Class of Americans Called Africans*, that subscriptions to the *Miscellany* "fell off to a ruinous extent,"[71] causing the magazine to cease publication in 1834.[72]

The major elements in "Jumbo and Zairee" were common to

115

much abolitionist writing. The decent though mistaken slave-holder, the cruel overseer, the disruption of slave families—these standard themes in antislavery fiction were echoed in those few children's stories which dealt directly with the issue.[73] The author of *Jemmy and His Mother* commented about slaveholders that "some of them are to be pitied for the great punishment that awaits them. . . . Many of them . . . cannot see they are doing wrong."[74] The overseer was the villain of *Walter Browning*, as he was of "Jumbo and Zairee," though in this story the plantation owner was also condemned as a man who thought of slaves "only in terms of money."[75] This 1859 tale treated very dramatically the separation episode so familiar in antislavery stories. When her child was sold away from her, the slave mother committed suicide by leaping from the boat which was carrying her away from the auction place.

But juvenile stories dealing with slavery, pro or con, were not at all typical of the bulk of the literature; children's fiction was seldom chosen as a vehicle for the heavy burden of the national debate over slavery. Undoubtedly influenced by practical considerations, authors, whatever their persuasions, avoided or softened the issue in their juvenile tales, and publishers usually acted on the *Youth's Companion* vow of "No sectarianism, no controversy."[76] The American conscience was increasingly tender on the subject of slavery, opinion splintered and sectional division grew ever deeper and more bitter as time went on. Publishers and authors who hoped to see their products widely sold walked carefully around those places where angels feared to tread.

On the whole, the social attitudes expressed in juvenile fiction were conventional and widely accepted in the period. Most authors subscribed in a general way to the democratic impulse of their time. Class attitudes were most evident in the authors' sensitivity to differences in manners and deportment, and a number of them seemed to be aware that there was here a possible contradiction of their professed rejection of social ranking based on anything other than "merit." Their answer to the difficulty was education: at home and in school, but especially at home, children of a democratic society should be so schooled in manners as to be able to take their places anywhere in society with ease. The other half of this argument was even more explicitly included in juvenile fiction: the children of the well-to-do, as much as the children of the "humble," should be brought up to be useful and practical, never idle and snobbish.

Most of the authors thought that the recent American past had maintained a higher moral standard than did the present; most were dedicated to restoring the moral tone of American society to those older standards. In their reverence for traditional values they were conservative. But much of the literature had a liberal side as well, as attitudes toward servants, toward the Irish, sometimes toward blacks, revealed.

Radical social ideas are rare in any literature written for children; certainly there were few in the antebellum juvenile fiction. Only a few of the multitudinous reform movements of the period appeared in children's stories, and those few were seldom seen in their most extreme form. Antiwar sentiment expressed by women and clergymen was acceptable enough, especially if it was not the radical doctrine of total nonresistance that was preached, but a milder form which opposed war as inhumane "in most cases," but admitted the necessity for self-defense or for war in a "just cause." Children's fiction commonly taught the moderate version of pacifism, though the reasoning about the decision to fight or not could be quite close.[77] Temperance, at least for children, was wholly acceptable doctrine, entirely free of the taint of radicalism. Antislavery, however, was a far more dangerous and divisive topic, as was sectarian religion, and both were generally avoided or treated with the greatest circumspection in children's stories. The social attitudes most unhesitatingly expressed in children's literature were those the authors considered most undeniably true, universal and uncontroversial, or those they held so deeply and so unconsciously that they thought of them not at all.

V

New Voices

"I hope it is funny, I hope there ain't any moral in it. Katy Smith's mother always puts a moral in; I don't like morals, do you, mother?"[1]

This remark, so openly addressed to a child's taste in stories, so casually subversive of the very foundation of children's fiction before 1860, places its source unmistakably in time. The speaker is a fictional child who has just asked her mother to tell a story, and the author is Sara Parton—"Fanny Fern"—but the voice is the voice of the 1850s.

The ten to fifteen years before 1860 saw new strains of fiction for children growing up beside the old varieties. Some of it was better literature, much of it was not; all of it foreshadowed the kinds of fiction that would flood the field of writing for children after the Civil War. The new fiction, usually by authors just entering the field was bolder, franker, sometimes more humorous and often more melodramatic, almost always more materialistic in its values, and more sentimental in its handling of problems than the old. The new authors were noticeably more concerned than the old to captivate their young readers and, to that end, paid closer attention to their tastes, as Fanny Fern demonstrated. They still larded their narratives plentifully with moral advice—in this respect, they had not really moved so very far from their predecessors or from Katy Smith's mother—but they buried their didacticism a bit deeper in adventurous tales, stories of dramatic encounters between noble youth and villains of various kinds, and stories of poor children rising meteorically in the world. They very often made certain of their audience by doing exactly that which William Cardell in 1825 had scorned to do; they made a story "more fascinating, by crowding it with incitements to eager curiosity or high wrought wonder." They used the "gaudy scenes" which he eschewed, and they apparently never worried, as he did, about the "mischievous" tendency of such literature for children.[2]

The new fiction departed in more than stylistic ways from the old. Content and concerns also shifted in subtle but significant ways. Emphases changed, old certainties wavered; the fiction at the end of the period spoke of a society grown more complex, less sure of its values, at once more aware of the recalcitrance of its problems and more inclined to escape them through sentimentality or melodrama.

The new writing did not, of course, immediately supplant the old. Even in the last years of the period, many stories were written for the young which exactly paralleled those of the 1820s and 1830s; indeed, many authors of the earlier years were still writing in the 1850s. But the movement to a different tone and point of view, just discernible in the mid-1840s, continued and accelerated to the end of the period, reflecting in fragmentary, oblique, and often belated ways some of the American responses to forty years of rapid social change.

William Taylor Adams, who wrote for children under the pen name of Oliver Optic, was a prototype of the new breed. Born in Massachusetts in 1822, a descendant of Henry Adams of Braintree, Adams had a public school education and two further years of private tutoring. He became a teacher, and later a principal, in the Boston public schools, where he remained for twenty years. Adams began writing juvenile novels in the mid-fifties and continued, very successfully, until nearly the end of the century. After a few books of fiction for children, Adams discovered a rich vein of popularity in the form of the series story, and in his lifetime produced many—the Great Western Series, the Lake Shore Series, the Yacht Club Series, and many others—most of them written after 1860. One of the early single stories, however, an 1854 juvenile novel entitled *Poor and Proud*, can serve as a showcase for many of the themes and attitudes which emerged in children's fiction in the latter years of the period.

The basic story of *Poor and Proud, or, the Fortunes of Katy Redburn* is quickly told, if some of the various subplots are ignored. As the story opens, Katy and her mother are in the direst poverty. Mrs. Redburn, the pampered daughter of a wealthy merchant, had defied her father's wishes to marry a poor clerk. At the time of the marriage, John Redburn was a good and noble young man, but he quickly degenerated into a "common sot" and reduced his little family to misery and want. While Katy was still very young, her father died of delirium tremens, leaving his widow to support Katy and herself as best she could by sewing. This she did until a few months before the time of the story, when she became ill and unable to work. Now she and Katy are entirely without food or money, the rent is overdue, and the hard-hearted agent for their landlady is threatening to evict them.

In the face of these daunting hardships, eleven-year-old Katy takes action. She tries to pawn her father's silver watch, but she is tricked by a dishonest pawnbroker. Dismayed but not discouraged, she goes to wealthy Mrs. Gordon, who owns the house in which she and her mother live, explains her situation and obtains not only a receipt for the month's rent, but a promise of help to get the watch back. Even more important, she favorably impresses this well-to-do lady, and henceforward has a benefactress.

Then enterprising Katy decides to go into business for herself, making and selling molasses candy. By hard work, perseverance and winning manners, Katy makes a success of her business—so much so, in fact, that she is able to expand, in true capitalist style, and employ other girls to sell the candy for a share of the profits. After a year of prosperity, however, the Redburn fortunes are once more reversed by Mrs. Redburn's illness. In desperate straits, Katy again repairs to Mrs. Gordon, this time to ask for a loan, offering the silver watch as security.

Now coincidence takes a hand in Katy's affairs and settles her financial worries forever. The inscription on the watch reveals that Mrs. Redburn is none other than Mrs. Gordon's long-lost sister, and thus heiress to part of the large fortune left by their rich father. All problems are resolved; Mrs. Redburn recovers her health, and she and Katy live in luxury at last, the candy business only a memory. In the last chapter,

Katy marries Tommy Howard, friend and protector of her early days who has also risen in the world from a cabin boy to captain of a clipper ship.

Poor and Proud was a lively tale, especially in comparison with stories of earlier years; Adams clearly had his attention fixed as much on his young audience as on their parents. It was not lacking in useful and moral lessons, however. As the title indicated, the major lesson of the tale dealt with right and wrong kinds of pride; it was possible to be poor and proud, the story taught, but pride must not be allowed to keep those who are poor from any sort of work which can support them. There was the usual plethora of minor moral messages as well, not all of them very well integrated either with the narrative or with one another; however, none of the moral teaching was allowed to get seriously in the way of the forward movement of Katy's story. Katy's rise in the world was the real point of Adams' tale, and he rarely lost sight of it for long.

The basic pattern of *Poor and Proud* was an early model of the stories of success and achievement which were to be so numerous in the 1860s and 1870s. The poor (but genteel) child is given the opportunity to display all the solid virtues of hard work, perseverance, courage, cheerfulness and pleasing manners in pursuit of a decent living. But real success comes about, not through laborious application to a lowly job, but through making a favorable impression on some wealthy person, or through sheer luck. In Katy's case, after she has had a suitable and improving struggle with poverty, amazing coincidence takes over and uncovers the relationship between Mrs. Gordon and Mrs. Redburn; in the well-known stories by Horatio Alger—and others—it is usually the patronage of a wealthy man or marriage with his daughter that makes the hero's fortune. In all cases, the virtues of the central character do not so much achieve his material success as qualify him for it.[3]

Indeed, the extreme social mobility so regularly depicted in the success stories of the 1850s served to emphasize the social conservatism of these authors. Since the degree of success achieved by the protagonists of these tales was such as to put them into the upper echelons of society, the writers had to ensure that they took their places with appropriate social ease and grace. Thus, as the authors wrote the American dream story over and over in the fictional histories of young persons who traversed great distances between poverty and wealth, they insisted, too, that their heroes and heroines be genteel whatever their initial poverty, well-bred, however straitened in circumstance, and socially equal to the best prizes that American opportunity could offer.

It is never difficult, therefore, to identify the child who is destined for success in any of these later stories. He will be well-favored, well-spoken, and well-mannered. Somehow his background, however deprived when the narrative begins, will have fitted him for a higher station in society. Katy Redburn, though she had herself known nothing but poverty in her life, had genteel manners and high ethical standards, presumably because of the tutelage of her mother, who was brought up in wealth and gentility. Alfred Raymond, hero of another success story of the 1850s, was also plainly marked for better things than the desperate poverty of his situation at the beginning of the narrative. Though nothing particular was said about Alfred's background, except that his mother had trained him in the Christian virtues, it was implied throughout that his poverty was an unnatural state for him. As things turned out, he owed his ultimate rise in fortune to wealthy benefactors who "instantly recognized" his superior qualities, all of which were conveyed through manners, speech, and other "class signals." By contrast, Alfred's friend and fellow newsboy, Bill Jones, was clearly lower class and just as clearly destined to remain in a lowly station, in spite of his good heart and "rough honesty." Again, the clues lie in his speech, manners and general bearing, which is rough, however honest.[4]

Realistically enough, most stories of spectacular rises in fortune had a city background. The setting for *Poor and Proud* was the city of Boston, a fact which was clearly, even vividly, given in the first pages:

The pier of the new South Boston bridge was then, as now, a favorite resort for juvenile fishermen. Flounders, tom-cod, and eels . . . used to furnish abundant sport to a motley group of youngsters, wherein the sons of merchants mingled democratically with the dirty, ragged children of the "tenfooters" of the vicinity.[5]

A city atmosphere pervaded the whole narrative, less because of detailed description—of which there was very little—than because Adams frequently mentioned street names, shops, alleys, the city hall, even a "piano-forte manufactory." He also imparted a sense of the variety of a city population—the "sons of merchants" and the "dirty, ragged children," the shopkeepers and the shop clerks, the servantmen who answered the doors of the well-to-do, and the mayor in his book-lined library.

Adams's use of a real and identifiable city as background was representative; cities were generally more visible in the late fiction than in earlier children's stories. But the old hostility toward them was by no means gone. Adams's portrait of Boston, while it suggested some of the less agreeable features of urban life, was on the whole a neutral picture; not all his contemporaries were as dispassionate. Even as they admitted the city to their stories, most authors regarded it with considerable misgiving. A city was a place of opportunity, to which they sent their fictional boys to make their fortunes, but it was also a den of wickedness, a place where temptation was rife, morality scarce, and high ideals constantly threatened.

Many tales with urban backgrounds portrayed city people as cold-hearted and morally irresponsible toward others. Alfred Raymond, orphaned at fourteen and nearly destitute, goes to New York to look for a job. There he asks an alderman to direct him to a hotel. The alderman indifferently sends the innocent boy to a rooming place next to a saloon: "Though one of the guardians of the city, he found no place in his heart for a poor boy. What was it to him whether or not the orphan boy went to destruction? He should get *his* salary." Alfred's encounter with the dangers of urban life does not end here. He wanders into the Bowery, where he is "befriended" by one of the "vicious poor," who takes him home, drugs him, and steals his money and clothes. When he escapes and is back on the street, sick, ragged, and penniless, the people of the city pass him by without regard. Even the policeman who orders him to go home responds unsympathetically when Alfred bursts into tears, explaining that he has no home to go to: "Go to the station house—that's the place for vagrants."[6]

Vagrants and thieves, venal officials and dishonest shop-keepers, and above all, the "vicious poor"—these hard-edged portraits suggest how the city had become a focal point by the 1850s for the anxiety of Jacksonian Americans over declining social morality and loosening social ties. Old simplicities were disappearing throughout the period, many Americans believed, and nowhere was their disappearance more apparent or more complete than in the fast-growing cities. "Human beings crowd together in cities and they teach each other tricks and devices to extort money, so that much care is necessary not to encourage worthless vagrancy."[7]

Concepts of poverty and charity were major victims of forty years of social change. Juvenile fiction of the 1850s revealed how far the ethical clarity of earlier years had given way in the face of social complexities. The duty of a Christian citizen toward the poor, once so plain, was now blurred and complicated by a myriad of considerations. The simple requirement to give to those in need nearly vanished, to be replaced by an ever more stringent insistence that the best charity consisted in "helping the character of the persons helped."[8] No longer did it suffice that "he is one of God's suffering creatures";[9] now it was necessary to judge whether charity might do him more moral harm than good, and, perhaps more important, how a partic-ular charity might affect society for good or ill. The duty to the poor was not revoked, but it was infinitely complicated by the necessity to avoid encouraging the idle in their idleness or the vicious in their vice.

To be sure, some prudence in giving had always been re-commended by practical-minded authors. To help in such a way as to aid the poor to become independent was best, Catherine Sedgwick and others had pointed out. But such observations in the earlier fiction centered upon the question of how best to help those in need, how to help them to help themselves, and never upon whether they should be helped at all. And the earlier authors, though they predicted that misguided charity might make the poor willing to remain dependent, rarely seemed to regard them with suspicion; there were no discussions of "tricks and devices" used by the poor to extort money. The acute concern with the "vicious poor" who deliberately deceived and dissembled to take advantage of Christian people was a new development in children's stories, which blanketed discussions of charity in the 1850s, especially charity to the urban poor.

The change involved only a slight shift in the angle of vision. It was an accepted axiom of children's fiction through all the prewar years that chronic poverty was unnecessary in the United States. Temporary poverty was an accepted fact of life; financial disaster could strike anyone, these authors often pointed out, so periods of poverty were nothing to be ashamed of. The poverty of the helpless—widows and children—also drew sympathy from most authors. But the poverty of able-bodied men or the willingness of any person—man, woman, or child— to take charity without trying to become self-supporting was not accepted at any time during the period, and remonstrances against such abuse of charity increased in the literature over the years. The United States was, after all, the land of opportunity; no one who wanted work need be without, no one who truly desired independence and respectability need be thwarted:

> Your existence is given to you in a land that may be called the *poor man's country*. In other countries people are driven by ignorance to vice, and by hunger to crime; but here instruction is offered to all; here labour calls out for hands; here ingenuity and perseverance are sure of reward; and here nothing but your own fault . . . can keep you from the society of the good and respectable.[10]

This reasoning applied to everyone. A thirteen-year-old girl, whose financial prospects were at the moment quite bleak, was told by her guardian that she should prepare herself for some work, for "many women you know support themselves entirely by their own works."[11] Another story commended an "ideot [sic] boy" for his moral character because, in spite of his handicaps, he earned some money and was not a charge upon the charity of others.

From the conviction that employment was possible for everyone who wanted it, it was but a step to the idea that chronic poverty and long-term dependence upon the charity of the respectable was the result of vice, laziness, or improvidence—moral failing, in other words. As time went on, this view was more and more often expressed in children's fiction, and in less and less compromising language: "In this land, . . . extreme want and the degradation of squalid poverty are generally confined to the vicious, the indolent and the grossly improvident."[12] T. S. Arthur's story, *The Beggars,* had a mother telling her children that no private charity was owed to the woman they saw begging with her three little children on a cold city street at Christmastime. She should have been "trying to support them [her children] with useful work" or, if that was impossible, she should "go to the Almshouse," for "idleness and beggary are next-door neighbors to vice."[13] Such sentiments were a long way from the stories of children giving pennies to poor people and finding satisfaction and parental approval in so doing, a long way from the simple 1823 advice to children that they are the "good and godly" who, "having much property, are moderate in their living and devote the surplus to charitable purposes."[14]

Suspicion did not always win the day against the charitable impulse. Some authors, as much aware as T. S. Arthur of the nefarious ways of the urban poor, still ended by recommending charity to their child readers. When Laura asked her aunt whether only good people should be helped, her aunt replied:

> By no means. . . . it is necessary often to relieve those
> whose vices have produced their misfortunes; but we must
> be very careful that our aid does not confirm them in those
> vices. We must do all that we can to induce self-help, and
> to keep them from wrong—which is the greatest of all
> misfortunes.[15]

But a chill of doubt had settled upon the discussion of charity;
even the most Christian giver had to take into account those
vices which may have produced the misfortunes he hoped to
relieve.

Ideals of private as well as public behavior began to show
alteration in many stories toward the end of the period. The
revisions were most apparent in the characterizations of family
and family relations, since these were so constant an element
in all juvenile fiction of the period. Katy Redburn's mother, for
instance, departed radically from the accepted standards of
former decades. The unfortunate Mrs. Redburn, reduced by
an imprudent marriage from wealth to want, evidently had
the sympathy of her creator, yet her behavior in the face of
adversity was in the sharpest contrast to that of ideal mothers
of earlier books. Those serene maternal models, whose eyes
were fixed on moral and spiritual values and who scorned to
complain of the material ups and downs of an imperfect world,
would never have exhibited such weakness and self-pity as
Mrs. Redburn did in telling Katy the story of her life: "Tears
blinded her eyes, and sobs choked her utterance, as she told
of the struggle she had had with poverty and want." They would
never have burst out so openly against cruel fate, especially in
the presence of their children: "It is hard to think how much I
have suffered!" And they surely would never have permitted
themselves the unmistakable materialism of her lament for the
loss of her father's wealth: "I suppose my father's property
must be in the hands of strangers, covering their floors with
soft carpets, and their tables with nice food, while I lie here
in misery, and my poor child actually suffers from hunger."[16]

Not mother, but child provided the model of character in

Poor and Proud. Though Adams pays an occasional compliment to Mrs. Redburn's rare moments of fortitude, it is Katy, rather than her mother, who is the source of strength for them both. Katy is a pillar of optimism and practical action; her mother leans upon her. "Don't cry, mother . . . I am going to take care of you now," Katy promises, and she does. Even when Mrs. Redburn fears the evil temptations to which Katy may be prey as she pursues her career of selling candy in the streets, she acquiesces: "Whatever views the mother had, there seemed to be no opportunity to carry them out, for by Katy's labors they were fed, clothed and housed. She was her mother's only support, and the candy trade, perilous as it was, could not be given up." Katy is always respectful, loving, and deferent in her manner toward her mother, but there is no mistaking the fact that it is she who leads, copes, and makes all the important decisions. There are even passages in which Katy undertakes correction of her mother's attitudes. In the course of the several pages it takes Katy to persuade her mother to let her go ahead with her molasses candy business, Mrs. Redburn deplores the kind of employment it will be. But Katy replies, "Do you remember the book my Sunday School teacher gave me last New Year's Day, mother? It was all about false pride; I want you to read it, mother. We can't afford to be so proud."[17] Such firm, plain leadership was of another order entirely from that of children of earlier tales who had led, if they led adults at all, by example alone.

The trend that moved the child to the active center of a fictional narrative also increasingly sentimentalized mothers and their ties with their children. Katy's impulse to "take care" of her mother was characteristic of the attitude of children toward their mothers in the new fiction. And the aura of pathos around Mrs. Redburn, while somewhat more pronounced than in most stories, was nevertheless representative.

All prewar children's fiction treated mothers with reverence, of course, but the standard relationship between mother and child in earlier decades was calm and unemotional. The ideal mother of those years was not only invariably controlled and rational toward the events of the outer world, but toward her children as well. She ruled through an affectionate but rather cool reasonableness. The good mother of the fifties was not necessarily so self-contained; her children might be called upon to protect or comfort her, and this they were more than ready to do, for their attachment to her was in some tales emotional and sentimental in the extreme. Between Mrs. Lenning and her children, Lewis and Charlotte, of *Get Money,* relations were fervid, to say the least. Lewis, meeting her at the train station, cried, " 'Mother, mother!' . . . from his overfull heart!" and lifted her in his arms. Lottie, when she saw her mother, "wept convulsively, for joy."[18]

William Adams did not give way to quite such overwrought sentiment between Katy and her mother, but he did include a scene in *Poor and Proud* in which Katy corrected a shop clerk's rudeness, gained her object (to sell candy in the store), and set the young man back upon the paths of righteousness, all by invoking the name of his mother: ". . . the allusions [Katy] had made to his mother burned like fire in his heart, for he had neglected her counsels, and wandered from the straight road in which she had taught him to walk."[19] The magic of the very word, "Mother," became a popular literary device in this late literature.

Fathers, on the other hand, were decidedly losing ground by the latter years of the period. Though they were rarely as prominent as mothers in earlier fiction, they were treated, when they were treated at all, with the greatest respect, unless they were drunken or dishonest. By the 1850s, however, fathers were being criticized more and more often for neglecting their families in favor of pursuing success in business. The "new pen" who wrote *Belle and Lilly* in 1857 described Lilly's father as "occupied only with money-making" and went on to show how unfortunate an effect this had on motherless Lilly and her little brother.[20] Mrs. Baker exhibited not one, but two unsatisfactory fathers in her 1859 collection of stories. One man of business, married to a woman who was entirely ineffectual in her domestic and maternal role, declined to take a hand in the management of his unruly household because, he said, he worked hard six days a week and was unwilling to "turn nurseymaid" on Sundays. The other father, Mr. Stephans, a widower and apparently an amiable gentleman, gave his children "everything but what they most required—a father's watchful care and instruction." Luckily, Mr. Stephans had the wit to marry an enlightened young woman who quickly reformed the entire family, not excepting her husband.[21]

Paternal failings were ever more varied as well as more frankly displayed as the period progressed. There were strong hints in some stories that fathers, even those who were not drunken sots, sometimes abandoned their families altogether. Lottie, of *Get Money*, admitted "with evident embarrassment" that her father was not dead, as the landlord had supposed, but had been "absent in a distant part of the country for several years."[22] The character weakness of Katy Redburn's father—which seemed to be vaguely attributed to his inconsequential origins—was painfully apparent in Mrs. Redburn's account to Katy of her father's descent into alcoholism. There were many overly indulgent fathers in the fiction of the 1850s, whereas earlier authors had generally seen excessive indulgence of children as a failing of mothers, which often had to be corrected by fathers.[23]

The cumulative effect of these more or less open assaults on men who were not fulfilling their duties as fathers was to elevate good women to positions of clear moral superiority over their husbands. Mr. Stephans was just one of a growing company of fictional men openly relegated to second place in households guided by women of lofty and impeccable ideals. Parallels with the popular domestic novel of the nineteenth century—and with the soap operas of the twentieth—are obvious, even where the parental roles were only background for the main story.[24] When an author moved the theme to the center of her story, as Mrs. Beale did in "Shadow in the House," the identity was complete.

"Shadow in the House" was one of two rather long stories written by Mrs. O. A. S. Beale and published together in 1859 under the title, *Georgy Lee*. Both narratives dealt with themes and lessons common throughout children's fiction in the period 1820 to 1860. But the melodrama and sentimentalism of Mrs. Beale's writing, and her glorification in "Shadow" of a model mother at the clear expense of a father who was neither alcoholic nor otherwise derelict, show her fiction closer to the woman-centered and sentimental domestic novel of the period than to most children's stories written before 1850.

"Shadow in the House" tells the story of the Mason family. Mr. Mason is a successful mechanic, "risen by industry and promptness to be one of the richest men in the young city of _____." Mrs. Mason is a perfect mother who knows the faults of her children, especially of her eldest son: "She had watched and corrected, as a mother only can, the faults of her eldest boy almost from his infancy. She had thrown about him all the enchantments of *home*; she had sought to draw him, by every art that affection could devise, to fix his thoughts to the lofty and good."[25]

But Herbert's character has somehow withstood all these affectionate assaults; he is not developing into an admirable boy. The major reason is that Mr. Mason does not cooperate with his wife in the moral training of their son. The boy is flattered by father, uncles, and grandfather, and soon he rebels against his mother's efforts to correct him. "Her influence was gone; her words were unheeded, so she wept in secret, and wondered what had caused the heart of her child to rebel against her government." As time goes on and Herbert grows worse, there is a degree of difference between his parents that would have been unthinkable in earlier stories. Mrs. Mason recognizes "more of her child's true character than ever before, and . . . the utter inability of the father to see and appreciate the subtle elements of his nature." A real breach opens between husband and wife when Mr. Mason believes Herbert's lying denials of wrong-doing rather than his wife's accusations. Mrs. Mason staggers "from the shock of being suspected of heartless conduct," and from being "treated as one whose opinions are to be cast away upon the idle winds."[26]

Herbert goes to live with his uncle, and almost immediately

commences a "street education." His mother, meanwhile, has begun to waste away. The denouement has Uncle Jerry discovering the truth about Herbert's evil ways; that "godlike woman," his mother, is vindicated at last. Mr. Mason is prostrate with guilt, as, indeed, are all who dared to think her wrong; but Mrs. Mason forgives him, "while a heavenly smile rested a moment upon her lips." Herbert, however, must suffer a bit more, in order that his character may be salvaged. His uncle keeps him from seeing his failing mother, reasoning that "the longer he was put off, the more he would appreciate his mother; if, indeed, she should be finally restored. The more he suffered for his sins the sooner he would forsake them; and although the tear of pity would often start in Uncle Jerry's eyes, he still felt a delicious satisfaction in Herbert's every pang." Herbert himself acquires a "slow fever" and begins to waste away, "but while his strength departed and his eye grew dim, his inner life was undergoing a most profitable and healthy change."[27] Nevertheless, having indulged herself (or her reader) in this kind of drama, Mrs. Beale suddenly rescues her characters from the jaws of death, reconciles them all with one another, and brings her story to a happy end.

Better than Adam's *Poor and Proud*, "Shadow in the House" represented the kind of melodrama and sentimentality which began to cross over from adult to children's fiction toward the end of the period. The differences in tone, feeling, and attitude between this and the great majority of earlier writing for children were broad but representative. The heightened emotionalism of the late stories barely served to obscure how much the faith in a reasoned approach to human problems had eroded by 1859. Mrs. Beale's solution to the central conflict of her narrative was sentimental in the extreme, a world away from the learning from experience and rational reflection favored in earlier stories. Mothers had sickened and died in many children's stories of the period, but their illnesses were not used to bring recalcitrant family members into line. Children learned through suffering in most antebellum children's stories, but in early books both their suffering and their learning were more conscious and more self-directed than Herbert's, and at least as much rational as emotional.

The entire narrative of "Shadow in the House" lacks that sense of conviction which was the backbone of earlier tales, even in those ideals and precepts which the author puts forth most didactically. Mrs. Beale quite evidently did not have the strong faith of her predecessors in the power of a good mother's influence to safeguard her children against all evil. Nor did she, apparently, trust the logic of events and the rationality of well-intentioned parents to work together to reform a wayward child. Certainly she had little faith in Herbert's conscience; it required an extreme threat of tragedy to bring him back to moral respectability.

The resolution of problems through emotional crisis, as in "Shadow in the House," or by coincidence, as in *Poor and Proud*, or through the intervention of wealthy benefactors, as in *Georgy Lee* and many others, was a hallmark of the new style of children's fiction. It suggested strongly that the new authors, though they ostensibly subscribed to much of the old code of belief concerning moral training and the ideals of child nurture, did not have as uncomplicated a faith in either the old methods or their goals as did their predecessors. And in fact, in their hands, the code was altered at nearly every point.

Goals were far more frankly materialistic than they had earlier been in children's stories. The definition of success and the reward of virtue were alike cast in material terms; the hero of a typical story of the fifties achieved an economic and social success well beyond that of most of his counterparts in earlier juvenile fiction. Where earlier writers had liked to see their heroes and heroines economically comfortable and socially respectable, the new writers wanted them resoundingly successful and socially enviable.[28] Mrs. Beale's orphan, Georgy Lee, did not simply become an "honored and respected member of society," in that favorite phrase of so many earlier books; he became a "great artist," rich and famous. One of many fictional newsboys rising in the world through honesty, ambition, and happy chance meetings with rich gentlemen who

133

offer jobs was James Horton. Instead of achieving merely modest security as a shop clerk or grocer, he ended as a "distinguished lawyer" with the "fire of genius" shining in his eye. And, of course, he and his mother prospered.[29] Lewis Lenning of *Get Money* was offered a partnership in the business of his first employer; by the end of *Poor and Proud*, Katy Redburn and her mother were living in "opulence."

The later fiction often made the connection between the practice of virtue and the achievement of economic advantage with a directness unprecedented in earlier children's fiction. It is hard to imagine a writer of the 1820s or 1830s rejoicing as openly in the financial reward of sterling character as did the author of *The Cooper's Son*. The hero of this story was falsely accused of wrong-doing by a "wilful, passionate, evil-minded boy," then cleared of the charge. The author exulted that Edward thus "not only triumphed over his enemies in vindicating his character, but he was to make a profitable job of it." The "best of the story," according to the author, was that the reward—a large sum of money—went to Edward, who used it to buy a house and farm for his mother.[30]

The latter 1840s and the 1850s also saw an ever-growing emphasis on what have been called the "employee virtues"—industry, punctuality, order, loyalty to employer, and the like—and these were now openly in the service of worldly success. While industry and orderliness had always been praised in children's stories, earlier writers generally spoke in favor of a child's industrious attention to his school lessons or to order in his tasks at home. For them, the good ordering of time was primarily to make room in life for both duty and pleasure; above all, it allowed one time enough to be "useful to others." Later attention to these good habits linked them specifically to business achievement, and business took precedence over most other claims, with the apparent approval of the authors. The model young man of *The Olneys* takes his leave of Mr. Olney saying, "Business before friends, you know." To which Mr. Olney replies with hearty accord, "Right, right. Order and punctuality are the wheels of business."[31]

Authors who so admired economic success obviously needed
to resolve some of the ambivalence toward wealth that haunted
earlier stories. And they did try. They still paid lip service to
the idea that ambition, and especially economic ambition, was
to be shunned. "Gold! The worst poison to the soul!" was
printed on the frontispiece of Mrs. Tuthill's *Get Money*, though
the story was a fairly representative sample of the popular
rise-to-riches tale. But the new fiction also created an image of
the successful businessman which the authors were prepared to
hold up to children as a model to admire and imitate. Mrs.
Tuthill's successful merchant, Moses Lawton, was typical. He
was "tall, erect . . . [with] an even row of well-kept teeth
. . . [his] expression mild and kindly." His mild and kindly
expression, however, masked an admirable firmness; his shop
was so run that "each clerk knew that in that place he must
mind his own business." He was a self-made man, of course,
who had earned his wealth, which was "immense." "Once a
poor boy, . . . Mr. Lawton made his immense fortune honest-
ly and honorably, and now spends it with the munificence of a
prince in a fairy tale, and at the same time with the good sense
and discrimination of a shrewd man of business."[32] Mrs.
Beale's self-made man showed just the same blend of firmness and charity: "Industrious as he was himself, he had no
sympathy for drones, and therefore was often called a 'hard
man,' while for the deserving and industrious his heart and
hand were ever open."[33]

In the new fiction, only honest men of busines prospered;
those who engaged in "sharp practices" sooner or later came
to grief. The new writers so cemented the causal relationship
between virtue and economic success that the older idea—always more implied than stated—that the practice of virtue
would ensure success, came to read in reverse: success implied
the practice of virtue.

Even the language of the new fictional style, which departed
from the sparse, restrained style of the old, signaled a change
in focus. The hyperbolic description of a young artist by his
benefactor was representative of a new concern with outward

traits romantically perceived and dramatically described: ". . . the burning brow, the flashing eye, and anon, the quivering lip and languid pulse."[34] The language was not realistic, but symbolic. A reader would not be likely to take tall, erect Mr. Lawton of the even, well-kept teeth for a villain, nor was he more likely to mistake the unattractive, crooked-toothed Mr. Ferguson of the same story for a hero—or, for that matter, for a successful merchant. And the use of such description also symbolized the generally stronger interest of a new generation of authors in the outer man, as against the preoccupation of the earlier authors with inward character alone.

Overall, in fact, the fiction at the end of the period showed a breakdown of the isolation so typical of most earlier stories. Juvenile literature began to take in more of the world outside the home; new social reality—however badly described or accounted for—appeared in as well as between the lines of the new fiction. Descriptions of poverty grew keener, sharper, less personal and more societal. In many of the later tales, poverty was less an affliction of one widow or one orphan, more a condition of a class of people, a level of society, than it had been heretofore. Patterned though they were, the accounts of urban poverty, Irish poverty, and the needs of poor children in the cities rang with the shock of discovery. Crime as an adjunct of poverty made its appearance; cities were no longer just full of vague "temptations" or "sin," but were more definitively hazardous, more clearly breeders and havens of crime, vice, and immorality. Five Points, the most notorious slum of New York, found a place in the literature.

At this same time, the melodrama and sentimentality so typical of adult popular literature throughout the period penetrated children's fiction, as though the strain of holding together a moral framework in an unpredictable world was suddenly too much for the old assurances. As a new generation of authors widened the compass of children's stories to take in more of the contemporary world, as their gaze moved from the inner conscience of a child and from largely spiritual rewards of goodness to outer circumstances that should proclaim the justice of Providence, they increasingly resorted to exaggerations of plot and feeling—and betrayed their doubt.

It was very much as though the reality and the materialism which had been pressing on the children's fiction all through these years had finally overtaken the traditional simplicities of moral faith and rational solutions. The moral certainty of earlier authors had rested in part upon moral abstraction and in part upon their conviction that an understanding of moral truth would work in its own time and way to produce a better world. The anxieties of the earlier years about conditions of Jacksonian society were largely expressed in their efforts to impart moral certainty to children at an early age. If this could be done, they suggested, then the disturbing anomalies of American life—selfishness, dishonesty, impersonality, and so on—would surely give way before the improved moral character of the next generation. The inevitable human suffering that remained—disease, death, and a certain degree and amount of poverty—would be tempered by human kindness and by spiritual recompense.

The realities of American social problems were hard on this vision. The problems stayed and grew, rather than diminishing and disappearing. Decades of American progress had not obliterated but increased poverty. Human indifference to the needs of others had not retreated under the assault of moral exhortation, but had grown as cities grew and communities changed. That glowing hope so characteristic of the earlier years that ideal home education would "[bring] back our guilty race to duty and happiness . . . [and] a new race of men would enter upon the busy scene of life, and cruelty and crime . . . pass away"[35]—such a faith was much eroded by the 1850s.

If children's stories had maintained a certain distance from social (though not personal) reality in earlier years, it was no longer possible to evade some awareness of the bitter realities of American life in the years just before the war. Time and history were closing in on problems of slavery, expansion, and sectional differences. Industrialization, immigration, and urbanization had worked together to produce problems of

137

urban and industrial poverty that blighted the optimistic American certainty that there would never be a "degraded class" in the United States. How could an author of children's books who lived and worked in New York or Boston avoid knowing of the frightful condition in which children of the urban poor grew up? It was not invisible behind factory walls. It was "children with no one to care for them, [who] spend their lives in the streets"[36] of New York; it was a child "so filthy, dirty—so ragged, that she scarcely looked like a human being."[37]

The new authors were less and less able to stretch the older faith far enough to cover these stubborn realities. They doubted that an easy conscience was ample enough reward for difficult virtue in a materialistic society, doubted that remorse would really punish the wickedly successful, doubted that individual Christian charity could meet the problems of growing urban and industrial poverty. They connected some of the moral problems of their time with broader causes than inept home nurture. Aldermen were corrupt and uncaring, so children in the city were swept into lives of vice for want of advice or protection.[38] Soulless technology, and even more soulless profit-gathering sacrificed the lives of innocent victims while an indifferent world spun on.[39] There was a new awareness of the corrupting effect of street culture, the lower-class urban environment which was sure to turn children into criminals or derelicts if they could not be removed from it, and a new uncertainty about the efficacy of individual charity as an ameliorative device. An understanding that problems of acute poverty and vice might have a broader social base than the faulty morality of individuals kept forcing its way into view even where some authors were clearly uncomfortable with the idea. The fragile edifice of moral certainty had been undermined by the environmentalism juvenile fiction had, itself, helped to foster.

The changed tone that distinguished one strain of children's fiction late in the period was surely both a reflection of and a reponse to such developments in American society over forty years. Melodrama and sentimentality had been part of American popular literature since the beginning of the century, but they were slow to appear in a children's literature soberly dedicated to the moral education of the rising generation. Their increasing frequency in the juvenile stories of the late forties and the fifties may be explained partly by evolving attitudes toward the uses of fiction by children. Some strictures had relaxed, and children's fiction began to be accepted more comfortably, less cautiously, as a source of entertainment as much as of instruction for children. True, the moral world had still to come out even in children's stories; good had to win, evil to lose, and no confusion was to blur the picture, but so was it also in nearly all the fiction written for adults. And if fiction was now somewhat freer to entertain children, as fiction entertained adults while it improved their moral sense, then some of the devices of adult fiction were permissible and perhaps even necessary in juvenile tales as in adult. Moreover, the devices had by now something of the patina of time and acceptance which is so reassuring to most of those who write for children. It seems likely that many authors who began their writing careers late in this period never paused to think, as so many earlier writers thought, that exciting narratives and emotional scenes were harmful to the young reader; they were simply the stuff of fiction.

At the same time, distorted plots and sentimental solutions to human problems in children's books suggested that the authors who used them looked at reality from another vantage point than did earlier authors. Their commitment to rational education was certainly less firm and less conscious. They could not, or at least they did not, draw so sharp a line between the moral education of a child and the adult experience of the real world; they found it harder to keep the two separated. Therefore, if rational thought and inner conscience did not succeed in making the adult moral world perfect—as they so clearly did not—they apparently found it difficult to believe that reason and conscience alone could foster moral certainty in children. Events must confirm the moral order of the universe and, as events unaided seldom obliged, authors had to pull and twist their plots to confirm the triumph of virtue and the downfall of vice.

Then, too, though they scarcely seemed to know it, many au-

139

thors of the 1850s had absorbed the materialism of their society sufficiently to alter quite basically the older notions about the proper goals of human life. Their stories consistently rewarded the practice of virtue with the achievement of a substantial economic success. This was not the mild and automatic material comfort of earlier stories, which had always been topped in any case by the satisfactions of a good conscience, but a triumph measured in strongly specific terms of wealth and fame. Many of the later stories revealed their authors' shift from the conservative tradition of middle-class Protestant values which emphasized piety and diligence in a worldly calling to that other strain in the American ideal of success which involved getting ahead through such qualities as aggressiveness, competitiveness, and enterprise in economic endeavor. Both ideals stressed success, but success was defined differently in each. For the older tradition, success was the achievement of respectability, competence in a calling, and salvation in the next world. For the second, the definition of success was almost entirely economic.[40]

But while the new authors of the fifties more or less openly accepted the second definition of success, they were still reluctant to endorse the aggressiveness and enterprise necessary to economic advancement in a competitive society. Those qualities, so frequently castigated in children's fiction throughout the peiod, were not yet acceptable in the literature. And so there yawned a considerable gap between ends and legitimate means.

Sentiment and drama could be used to fill the space; they could legitimize pecuniary success and take the hard edge off economic ambition. Thus, Katy Redburn demonstrated a high degree of initiative and economic enterprise in her story, but the necessity for it had to be established by the sentimentally desperate poverty she and her mother were suffering. And in the end, though Katy did well in her business venture, it was melodramatic and improbable coincidence that brought about the decisive attainment of "opulence," and so at once salvaged her character from the blemish of crass economic ambition and awarded her an enviable return for virtue and effort.

But most of all, the emotionalism, sentimentality, and theatricality of many later children's stories seemed to be an effort by the authors to insist upon the moral order of the universe when the world more immediately around them was increasingly, inexplicably chaotic. The change was not complete by the end of the period; the old and the new lived side by side in children's books for many years. Yet, the pace of political events and the recalcitrance of social problems in the United States of 1820 to 1860 accumulated relentlessly, always increasing the strain on that precarious moral certainty by which earlier generations had held together the ideal and the real. The new authors clearly lacked the iron-clad faith of their predecessors in the ultimate justice dealt out by God and conscience, yet they clung to the old code of values, paying lip service to it even as they altered it, invoking ever more unlikely luck, coincidence, and a kind of secular Providence to make things come out right. The new fiction portrayed the outer world more completely, more vividly, and in some ways more realistically than the old, but its emotional tone was less confident and less trusting. The fictional solutions to social and moral problems in the new literature were no less simplistic than those of the older tales, and in some ways they were far more irrational. It is hard to avoid the conclusion that the more the authors of children's fiction turned their attention to the outer world, the more they were overwhelmed by what they found there, and the more they resorted to the artificial solutions and escapism of melodrama and sentiment.

VI

"By the Fate of Carthage"

The years between 1820 and 1860 were remarkable even in American history for their phenomenal rate of change. Every aspect of American life was moving, growing, shifting; the ferment of the age can hardly be exaggerated. Physical expansion was enormous; the frontier moved across the continent from the Mississippi Valley to the edge of the Pacific. The acquisition of Texas alone added territory larger than that of the thirteen original states to the nation. Eleven new states were admitted to the Union during these years.

The growth of the population was scarcely less impressive. In forty years, the number of Americans increased by well over 200 percent. Natural increase accounted for much of the added population, but immigration also contributed. Some five million immigrants came to the United States between 1820 and 1860, most of them in the latter twenty years of the period. They brought with them customs and mores new and sometimes unsettling to "old stock" Americans, and so contributed to the dynamic atmosphere of change and resistance to change that characterized the era.

Not least, this was the period in which that most characteristic development of modern nations, industrialization, began to make significant inroads upon American life. Especially in New England and the Middle Atlantic states, the rate of manufacturing growth before 1860 was extraordinarily rapid. Developments in transportation and the introduction of machinery into the production of goods transformed the character of everyday life in the United States. Nine thousand miles of railroad were built before 1850; twenty thousand more were added between 1850 and 1860. By the end of the period, machinery dominated the manufacture of many products—textiles, glass and iron, among others—and even agriculture, the occupation of most Americans in these years, was substantially altered by 1860 from an entirely human effort to a machine-assisted form of labor.[1]

Political and social change accompanied the physical and technological development of the period. Marvin Meyers has pointed out far along the course of democratization the United States had come by the election of Andrew Jackson.[2] Property requirements for suffrage were fast falling as early as 1820; universal suffrage for white male Americans was an accomplished fact for most of the period. Increased political democracy changed the complexion of American politics. National parties developed which paid court to the "common man" who now had the vote, rotation in office and increased numbers of elective offices made political activity virtually constant. Politics was every man's avocation.[3]

The period was socially and politically, as well as economically, an age of opportunity. Class lines, always flexible in America, became even more fluid. The hopes of most Americans were high, and few rigid class barriers stood in the way of those who bettered themselves economically and professionally. Perhaps the most visible element of the social climate, in fact, was that expectation Edward Everett Hale described, "of a speedy improvement, not to say revolution, in social order, such as men do not often experience. . . . The country was prosperous; [Americans] were prosperous, and they looked forward to a noble future."[4]

The expectation of a "noble future" contibuted to the passion for reform that filled the Jacksonian era with hope and unrest. There was at least one cure, and often more than one, for every social and human ailment. Religion became man-centered, and at the heart of evangelical religious doctrine, as at the center of much secular thinking, was a belief in the perfectability of man. This, together with an evangelical activism, loosed an astonishing energy for reform. Concern over the ills of society coincided with hope for the future of man in crusades against slavery, intemperance, and war. Humanitarian and moral reformers assailed most of the ancient afflictions of mankind, including crime, poverty and ignorance, in the belief that moral conviction and human industry could best them all.[5]

Tradition has usually pictured the response of Jacksonian Americans to the remarkable developments of their era as confident, nationalistic and optimistic, and in broad outline, the characterization is doubtless accurate enough. The rhetoric of the time was often exuberant; public pronouncements were full of nationalistic fervor, celebrating American growth, American freedom, American institutions. Jacksonian commentators often equated change with progress[6] and certainly by any such definition, the United States was moving forward at a startling pace. Most Americans were caught up in the momentum of their country's extraordinary growth. They responded to the apparently unlimited opportunities of their time with an enthusiasm and hunger for success that gave the period the gloss of optimism for which it has been known.

But rapid social change exacts a high price from human beings, and Jacksonian Americans were not exempt from the toll. Recent scholarship has located a strong current of doubt and anxiety running beneath the characteristic buoyancy of the period. Americans were unprepared, as Marvin Meyers has noted, for the "grinding uncertainties, the shocking changes, the complexity and indirection of the new economic ways."[7] The breathtaking rate of growth that occasioned so much self-congratulation among Americans also broke apart families and communities, dissolved the bonds of tradition and created a population of restless people whose ambition drove them to an unceasing search for they knew not what—success, fame, money, or perhaps, only more change. The dominant forces of the time were expansive and their effect was correspondingly centrifugal. American life had a minimum of structure and a maximum of freedom; the question was how to reconcile freedom with order, how to keep ambition from trampling all other values underfoot, how to work out the American destiny without sacrificing all traditional values in the name of the future. The people of the United States believed in progress, and were proud of the advances they made, but they also felt keenly the threat that new ways posed to older values they cherished.

Twentieth-century social observers, themselves amply familiar with the phenomenon of extreme social change, have pointed to alienation as one direct result of living with rapidly shifting values. Margaret Mead and Kenneth Keniston, to name only two, have attributed the alienation of many twentieth-century Americans to the bewildering rate at which society in this century has changed and continues to change. Constant social change, they have pointed out, tends to loosen the ties of the individual with even his own history; mobility is paid for with loneliness.[8]

Tocqueville saw symptoms of anxiety and alienation in the Americans of the 1830s. The democratic man as he described him then was a lonely being, driven by unappeasable ambition. He was free, to be sure, but he was adrift in an atomized society that offered no frame to hold his life: "Not only does democracy make every man forget his ancestors, but it hides his descendents and separates his contemporaries from him; it throws him back forever upon himself alone and threatens in the end to confine him entirely within the solitude of his own heart."[9]

And, though to most Americans, the ambition and opportunism of their fellow citizens was more apparent than the doubt, the anxiety did not altogether escape contemporary American notice. While most Jacksonians called themselves a "fortunate people" of a nation "most blessed on earth," an 1836 report of the New York State Medical Society observed, "The population of the United States is beyond that of other countries an anxious one. All classes are striving after wealth, or endeavoring to keep up its appearance. . . . we are an anxious, care-worn people."[10]

The fiction for children that arose in the Jacksonian years was a testimonial both to the optimism of the period and to its anxieties. The very existence of the literature attests the intense concern with childhood and child-rearing which was one facet of the American response to the developments of early nineteenth-century society. Americans felt keenly how dependent their democratic nation was upon the good character of its citizens; at the same time, they were deeply apprehensive about the pressures and temptations inherent in an expanding, ambition-driven society. Only the strongest character could meet the challenges of such a time, they felt; only the firmest principles would hold in the swift currents of change. Childhood, therefore, was a crucial time during which children were to be molded to desirable habits as a preparation for responsible citizenship. It was not to be wasted in trivial pursuits, nor squandered on merely fashionable accomplishments. It must be used to fit the rising generation for the future.

But childhood was brief in America before 1860. Not for long, as Tocqueville noted, were the children of the United States dependent upon their parents, and when they took their fortunes into their own hands, their independence was complete; no strong or extended family ties held them within the orbit of parental influence.[11] The family role in the making of an American was consequently sharply limited in time, yet it was emotionally and socially central. Amid the ceaseless fluctuation of Ameri-life in these years, the family was the stable point: "The family was the one substantial social institution in a nation that had discarded hierarchial religion and . . . reduced government to a minimum, while business corporations had not yet attained notable development."[12] As the structure of society became ever more flexible, as community mores changed both obviously and subtly, the family was more and more heavily charged with the main responsibility for conveying traditional values to the children of the republic.

Children's fiction developed as an adjunct to this essential family function. All literature for children in this period built upon the conviction that a child's early training was the most decisive single influence upon his character, and the fiction written for children was especially and explicitly dedicated to reinforcing the standards of ideal home training. Like exemplary home education, juvenile fiction concentrated on character development, and proceeded through exhortation and illustration to present to children a firm set of standards to guide them when parental guidance ended. Like most theories of character training in the period, the fiction also conveyed a sense of urgency about the uses of childhood, insisting that principles must be inculcated early before the temptations of the world could erode a child's inclination to be good. The didacticism of the stories was a logical outgrowth of the assumptions about the function of literature in a child's life. Behind the didacticism was the palpable fear that a child not well prepared by moral education would quickly succumb to the evils of the unstable world beyond the home.

In content as in intent, children's fiction represented both the hopes and fears of its times. The fears, however, were nearly always more evident than was the optimism. Writers did pay some tribute to the promise of American life. Some, like Catherine Sedgwick, named some of the advantages and opportunities of their democratic society—the free public education, the absence of rigid class barriers, the availability of employment to all who wanted it. But, as was perhaps inevitable in a hortatory literature, it was the anxieties of the authors about their society and its dislocations that shone with greatest clarity through the thin narratives and the moral preaching. Writing as they did for wholly didactic purposes, the authors stressed the virtues they thought most threatened, and warned against those faults they found most threatening. In their choice of what to praise and what to blame lie clues to the response of these writers to their changing society.

They approved obedience, submissiveness, kindness and charity. They believed in settled virtues: home, family, rural living, contentment and predictability. They preferred order and utility over creativeness and intellectuality, and safety over adventurousness. Generally speaking, they lauded the past more than the present. Above all, the stories they wrote were suffused with a desire for moral certainty which entirely superseded any other considerations. These stories sacrificed any sense of the complexity of their age in order to preserve perfect moral clarity.

They were equally agreed on what they condemned. Selfishness was the primary sin in children's fiction, and its bad name covered a variety of faults. Ambition was deplored, and every

147

form of aggressive self-will. Unkindness or indifference toward others was chastised, as was snobbishness or other evidence of setting worldly values above "true merit" or goodness. The moral weakness of drunkards, liars or those who could not hold to principle in the face of temptation was anathema to writers of juvenile fiction, who clearly found such pliability alarming.

Even the simplest catalogue of good and bad as defined in children's stories suggests that these writers were reacting against the turbulance, the competitiveness, the individualism of their era. The fictional ideal embracing self-discipline, respect for authority and orderly personal habits, and repudiating "restless striving" and "selfish ambition" was a reverse image of the realities of Jacksonian America as most contemporary observers described them.

No trait, for instance, was more frequently praised in the fiction than obedience to parents, none more consistently condemned than disobedience. Yet foreign visitors who recorded their impressions of American family life rarely found American children obedient. On the contrary, they usually described them as "independent" or even "precocious," and frequently suggested that their manners toward their elders were less respectful than they should have been.[13] The authors themselves occasionally admitted the reality of disrespectful American children. "Much as I love children in general," remarked Lydia Maria Child, "there is nothing so distasteful to me as a froward [sic] child."[14] And Samuel Goodrich complained of children "who think they can go anywhere, and do anything, in their own way, and without any guide."[15] Obviously, the enormous emphasis on obedience in children's stories was addressed to a felt need; the obedience of American children could not be taken for granted.

Just as clearly, there was more at stake in these tales of the rewards of obedience and the perils of disobedience than simple correction of childish waywardness, or even the enforcement of a basic respect for parental authority. The wider implications were sometimes spelled out when an author made specific the link between a child's obedience to his parents and the preservation of the larger social order, as did the writer who pointed out that "the obedience of children to their parents is the basis of all government."[16] More often the tie was left implicit, but it was seldom hard to discern the authors' fear that disruption of the proper relations within a family was the first step toward the disruption of all reasonable order in society. If the family was the primary basis of social order, it was also a last stand against continually shifting social standards. In the home, the stories said, a child must learn order, for there may be no other place for him to learn it. There he must acquire a decent respect for authority, or he will flout it everywhere, to the detriment of all social relations. The good order of American society was forfeit to a disobedient child.

Similarly, docility, that virtue so often extolled in children's stories, had implications beyond and beside its apparent meaning. Like obedience, docility, or "submissiveness," would seem to have been a trait not conspicuously typical of American children in this period. Visitors to America were more likely to comment upon the self-assertiveness of Americans, including children, than upon their docility. Children's fiction, however, regularly lauded submission and promised that this quality, so at odds with the apparent requirements of a competitive society, was a key to true happiness.

The discrepancy between the ideal of docility and the reality of American society suggests both the special ways in which the word was used and the function this virtue was assigned in American life. The concept of docility, or submissiveness, as it existed in the stories had little to do with a meek bowing to authority. Instead, the term brought together two themes that ran through most of the fiction: self-discipline and unselfishness. Submissiveness meant putting the wishes (not the commands) of others ahead of one's own. It meant the strict schooling of every self-centered impulse, and the deliberate subordination of all spontaneous desires to the wants of others. It set out an ideal of selflessness that went well beyond ordinary kindness or thoughtfulness toward a high degree of self-denial.

The level of self-abnegation required by this ideal was hardly a realistic goal for anyone, and it was perhaps especially unrealistic for children. But realism was not the point. The concept of living totally "for others" existed to counterbalance the selfishness the authors found all too evident a reality of their time. Many Americans of the period felt their society dissolving into an agglomerate of individuals, each pursuing his own ends, indifferent to his fellow man at best, in savage competition with him at worst. If the condemnations of selfishness and the lauding of docility so common in children's fiction are read in the right light, the aggressiveness and competition of Jacksonian society, otherwise strangely absent from the literature, begin to appear between the lines. What Tocqueville viewed as the democratic danger of individualism—the spirit of every man on his own and for himself—the authors of children's stories saw as a rampant selfishness whose unchecked growth could ultimately destroy all semblance of social decency and cooperation in American life.[17]

The pure selflessness recommended in children's stories was thus the mirror image of the total selfishness the authors so much feared, and the high pitch of the ideal was a measure of the need and the uncertainty of such standards. These writers wanted to believe that such disinterestedness was humanly possible because they believed that it was imperative if American society and social decency were not to be entirely engulfed by greed and competition.

"Selfishness" stood for almost everything these writers deplored in their own society, but it especially indicated the author's mistrust of the ascendancy of individualism. Disobedience in children seemed to be the symbol for all disruption of social order, in families or without. "Fashionableness" represented the abandonment of traditional values for new styles of living, styles which most of these writers found less sober, industrious and responsible than the old. Literary cries against the coldness of charity or the indifference of those well-to-do who neglected the less fortunate around them suggest how distressed these writers were over the growing impersonality of their era. Fictional tales of young men who abjured distant opportunity to seek their fortunes close to home revealed their dismay over the rootlessness that was increasing as the American population spread out to fill a growing nation.

In short, anxiety permeated the children's fiction of this period, appearing between the lines and in the form of warnings and admonitions of various kinds. Specific areas of anxiety—the false values of pecuniary success, the cities that bred crime and immorality, alcoholism, indolence, parental neglect of children—often blended into vague, fundamental misgivings about society, and found expression in disapproval of childish misbehavior.

Yet in spite of their apprehensive reaction to many of the developments of their time, the authors of antebellum juvenile fiction were not conservatives who set themselves against all change. Their writing was an amalgam of old and new social concepts, conservative and progressive attitudes. They were rarely systematic thinkers. Some few, like Jacob Abbott, developed a comprehensive philosophy of child training, but most merely borrowed and adapted the notions that were in the air during those years.

The broad generalization that would cover the majority of these writers is that they were progressive in their attitudes toward the nature of childhood and methods of child nurture, and conservative in their social and moral values. A degree of cultural lag is normal in most children's literature. Adults tend to be conservative about passing on to children new and untried social or moral concepts; not until they have been worn somewhat smooth with use and acceptance will social ideas normally enter children's books.

Thus, though nearly all authors of antebellum juvenile fiction seemed to have abandoned the Calvinist idea of the depraved nature of children, they handled the subject by implication, rather than by avowal. They engaged in no discussions of the balance between good and evil in a child's inborn character, but their view of children was tolerant. They expected faults and imperfections, and they usually did not take the natural failings of childhood as evidence of innate wickedness. Although they regarded all moral missteps with gravity, most of these authors evidently believed that a child's native impulse to be good was as strong as any tendency toward evil. If the extreme optimism of Transcendental and romantic thinking about the perfectibility of man was missing from children's fiction, there was also little pessimism. During most of the period, the moral arguments lacked the kind of stridency that often signals despair.

Most authors believed in a reasoned approach to child training. They deplored harsh and punitive methods, convinced that child nature included enough rationality to make discussion and meditation effective means of correction. Most openly repudiated physical punishment, and some pointed out that it "warped and blunted" a child's moral feelings.[18] Such attitudes put these writers in tune with the domestic reform efforts of their time;[19] at the same time, they expressed an older faith in rationality that had begun to give way on the adult level to a romantic preference for emotion over reason. Only in the last ten or fifteen years of the period did romanticism become a major strain in children's literature which was discernible in a generally increased sentimentality, and especially in the tendency of some of the later authors to substitute sentimental feeling for rationality as an instrument of family discipline.

Throughout the period, the didactic arguments in much of the fiction were plagued by a contradiction, usually unacknowledged, between the authors' notions of environmental influence on human behavior and their desire for moral certainty. Many writers of juvenile literature occupied an uneasy transitional position between the progressive view of human failing which looked to environmental causes, and the traditional acceptance of a strict individual moral responsibility. Most were committed, by logic as well as conviction, to the idea that environmental influences—the standards of home, the matter and the manner of a child's upbringing—were primary in determining his character and behavior. They were thus willing to concede that the responsibility of an ill-taught child for bad behavior could not be equal to that of the child who had the advantages of a moral education. "A girl who has a selfish, indolent mother, devoted to fashion and vanity, must not be judged as we should judge one whose mother was like Catherine's"—that is, enlightened, rational and diligent in the education of her daughter.[20]

But such tempering of moral judgments led forthwith into very troubled waters indeed. Who was then properly responsible for wrong-doing by a child? The child? His parents? The society? As Americans became increasingly familiar with the problems of chronic, many-generation poverty, mostly through the example of Irish immigrants whose opportunities in the old country had been nonexistent and whose ignorance and poverty perpetuated their miseries in America, such environmental explanations became both more apparent and more dangerous. The solution for the children of such parents, many thought, was to remove them from their hopeless surroundings. "There was hope for the children, if, while young, they could be removed [from idle, shiftless, parents]."[21] And it became the mission of many social reformers to do just that: to provide an alternative, institutional or otherwise, to homes whose influence they thought could only be baleful.[22] But what of the many never reached by Sunday School teachers, foster homes, or institutional care? How was their responsibility for their behavior to be judged if they had never been exposed to proper teaching? And if wrong-doers were to be excused from judgment when they had not been taught right and wrong, what then became of individual responsibility? What became of a democracy, dependent upon responsible citizens?

These writers did not grapple with such questions in the fiction they wrote for children, any more than they debated other philosophic questions, but the potential contradictions between their environmentalism and their strong commitment to personal responsibility haunted the stories. One Sunday School Union writer saw where the logic of environmental thinking led, and rejected the view that saw a criminal "as a victim to be pitied rather than as an offender to be punished." He thought such a theory would destroy "all motive for exertion, and excite bitterness and envy against the more prosperous."[23]

But Maria McIntosh was more typical. On one page of her story, *Ellen Leslie*, Ellen's uncle gave the customary tolerant description of the faulty heroine: "I must not let you suppose that our little Ellen has no good in her. She is . . . a very affectionate child . . . though she is so ready to fancy herself neglected and ill-treated. . . . It is [her parents'] fault. She has been spoiled from her very birth." Nevertheless, only two pages later, Ellen's kindly relative held her to account: "I think that

153

everyone should bear the consequences of their own faults."[24] There could be no comfortable resolution of this conflict for a society caught between a growing comprehension of the social bases of behavior and a system of moral and social value ultimately dependent upon a concept of individual moral responsibility.[25]

However enlightened the methods underwritten in most children's fiction, they were generally in the service of traditional goals. The authors consciously embraced the virtues of the "good old catechising, school-going, orderly times."[26] It was an axiom of the literature that Americans of times past had embodied all the virtues recommended for young readers. The Revolutionary generation especially appeared in the fiction as the model of total dedication to the interest of community and country, proof that such standards were attainable and demonstration of the great benefits that accrued to all society from the lofty character of individual citizens. As their idealization of the past plainly indicated, these writers considered that child behavior had fallen off badly since Revolutionary days. What they hoped to achieve through rational child nurture was a return to the standards of obedience and order which they were sure had prevailed in earlier generations, and which they were equally sure had provided the foundation of the principled character of earlier society.

Yet the didacticism of the literature was not simply an effort to shape children's behavior to conform with some authoritarian or "puritanical" idea of how children should behave, nor to make life more comfortable or convenient for adults. The moral earnestness of the literature as a whole went well beyond such superficial motives. The children the stories presented as ideal images were no automatons programmed to do as they were told without question or reflection. Nor were they children "seen but not heard," encouraged to behave so as to be a minimum of trouble to their elders.

On the contrary, ideal fictional children were thinking and reflecting beings deeply engaged—with the constant aid of their rational parents—in the examination of moral values, and in the development of the strength of character to act upon their convictions of the right. Most children's authors made it apparent that overt behavior was not at all the sole target of the plentiful moral instruction in their stories. The insistence upon examination and judgment of the impulses behind action, good as well as bad, made it clear that it was motive, not just behavior, that most writers hoped to affect. Right *feelings* were what mattered most: the authors wanted to bring children to what they called the "correct view" of every moral situation. Their most serious attention was directed to the development of the moral sense of the American child—that child who was the "pivot of the moral world."[27]

It was this fundamental assumption about the significance of individual behavior that gave an otherwise limited literature a certain dignity. E. Douglas Branch's criticism of the antebellum age, that it wanted "religion without humility . . . benevolence without sacrifice . . . salvation without pangs,"[28] has been applied by Herbert Ross Brown particularly to the popular literature of the period. But such a charge cannot fairly be brought against most of the juvenile fiction. While children's literature certainly shared many of the flaws of adult popular fiction, these moral equivocations were not typically among them. To be sure, not all authors were equally sincere in their commitment to the concept of moral responsibility; the field had its share of hack writers who simply adopted the conventional moral and educational stance of their era and put it to use in numberless volumes of shallow moralizing and instruction. And sincerity did not make artists of even the most earnest writers: the moving aspects of the tales usually reach the reader in spite of, rather than because of, their literary quality.

Yet the steadfast belief of most authors in the reality of moral choices and in their importance, both for the individual who made them and the society of which he was a member, weighted their slight narratives. William Dean Howells, writing in 1890 of his boyhood in the forties, described the part that religion played in the lives of his parents: "It was simply a pervading influence; and I am sure that in the father and mother it dignified life, and freighted motive and action here with the significance of eternal fate."[29] This was the role that moral seriousness played in the juvenile fiction of the period.

Changes toward the end of the period carry their own message. The gap between the ideal and the real widened, and the efforts of the new generation of writers to bridge it became at once more desperate and more conscious. Ostensibly, the values later authors espoused were not different from those of earlier writers. They still claimed moral principle as the only true basis of happiness, refused to accept openly worldly ambition, and declared their faith in the ultimate ascendancy of good over evil.

But the melodrama and sentimentality that saturated much of the literature of the 1850s suggested that there was growing doubt, not about the value of moral ends, but about the processes of achieving them. Early and late, juvenile fiction tried to account for the apparent success of selfishness, dishonesty, and "sharp dealing." Precisely because they could not avoid recognizing how often the good seemed to suffer in spite of their moral worth, how frequently the wicked, the ruthless and the immoral seemed to have their way and escape the consequences, how often, in brief, the moral world seemed out of joint, the authors of children's books tried to right the balance by insisting that the true measure of human contentment could not be taken from these outer manifestations. Early writers insisted that the happiness of the wickedly successful was an illusion; God and human conscience would see that the wicked suffered and that the good knew the true joy of inner contentment: "the vicious shall not prosper."[30]

The impression is strong in most stories published before 1850 that the authors were able to believe in their concept of ultimate moral balance. While the injustices of the real world undoubtedly troubled them, there was in their writing a fundamental serenity that bespoke a strong faith in the spiritual justice of the universe. But the new authors who began to write in the late forties and fifties seemed less certain, less calm. They righted things more dramatically and more materially in their stories. Their dishonest merchants failed in business: "dishonesty is the worst policy."[31] Dramatic illnesses, fortuitous meetings, unmaskings of villainy—these, rather than the slower workings of time and conscience were the instruments of moral justice in the late fiction. The moral world had to be put right, but the new writers were not content with the old spiritual assurances. They cared more about the unfairness of the worldly system of rewards and punishments, perhaps because the realities of their time were so inescapable, certainly because they more thoroughly accepted the material measure of their own society, and surely too because they were less convinced that the good were in fact happy within their own hearts and that the wicked were correspondingly miserable. Unable to keep the sphere of home and child entirely clear of their doubts about the unpredictable moral world, they resorted to the kind of contorted plots and exaggerated feeling that had characterized adult popular literature since the beginning of the century. Behind their sentimental solutions to problems, one senses a desperation, if not a despair, not common in earlier juvenile stories. Undoubtedly they thought they were presenting to children the same view of a morally orderly universe that the earlier fiction had always upheld; in fact, a modern reader discerns their doubts.

Whatever the shifts of form and faith, however, the typical fictional work for children throughout the period remained a work of moral drama. However circumscribed the point of view, however plodding and mundane the action, however small the scale, and even in the distorted melodramas of the end of the period, the heart of nearly every story was the eternal struggle between good and evil in the conscience of a human being.

Horace Bushnell's concept of spiritual education, set out in his philosophic treatise, *Christian Nurture*, could stand as well for the theoretical statement of the structure inherent in children's fiction. Though he was neither Calvinist nor pessimist, Bushnell believed in the reality of evil, and could not accept the kind of contemporary optimism that seemed to deny it. He believed that spiritual education required what he called an "experiment of evil"—a "struggle with evil, a fall and a rescue." The attainment of maturity he thought demanded "a double experience . . . of] the bitterness of evil and the worth of good."[32]

Most writers of children's books before 1850 had anticipated him. They, too, understood that "the growth of Christian virtue is no vegetable process, no mere outward development."[33] The experiment of evil, the struggle, fall and rescue—above all, the discovery of "the bitterness of evil and the worth of good"—was the fundamental and nearly invariable plot of the children's stories. The child who learned that her own happiness depended upon what she did for others was learning the worth of good.[34] The boy who took cherries from his father's tree and was branded a thief—for several years—by all who knew him, surely learned the bitterness of evil.[35] All the tales of disobedience repented, temptation overcome, and happiness and success awarded to the virtuous, followed the outline of Bushnell's spiritual education. A belief in the reality of both good and evil was the backbone of the juvenile literature. Every writer of children's fiction wrote morality plays.

And something more. There was a curiously dark side to the literature as a whole, an edge of fear that was sharper than mere dissatisfaction with changing social conditions. Through the excess of caution, the emphasis on order and stability, the insistence that the key to social peace lay within the individual, the fiction conveyed a sense of catastrophic alternative to personal and social decency. "Doom!" said D. H. Lawrence, "haunts all of American literature,"[36] and even here, in these slight and purposeful tales, its shadow fell.

It would overburden a very slender literature to suggest that the children's books prophesied doom, even indirectly. But the call for order, self-control and discipline, repeated again and again in every story, did echo a dread of disorder, an apprehension the individual loss of control would end in social disruption at best, in total disintegration at worst. It was a fear the writers shared with many other Americans of their time. Nathaniel Hawthorne conjured up a terrifying vision that seemed to gather together all the vague uneasiness of the era: "Where is our universe? All crumbled away from us; and we, adrift in chaos, may hearken to the gusts of homeless wind, that go sighing and murmuring about, in quest of what was once a world."[37]

Nothing in juvenile fiction was as powerfully written, as horrifyingly specific, as that, but there was nevertheless a strong emotional kinship between this haunting passage and the cumulative sense of apprehensiveness that pervaded the children's literature. A horror of social breakdown hovered behind the endless admonitions to children to be strong in moral principle and steadfast in meeting temptation. A fear that democratic freedom might mean the end of all restraint on individual rapacity intensified insistence on the duty to care for the fate of others. The old Puritan concern that man in the wilderness would revert to ignorance and barbarity found an echo in the nineteenth-century fear that man in a competitive society would become a moral savage and so reduce his world to chaos. The children's stories of 1820 to 1860 were written, in fear and in faith, to salvage the American future from such a possibility.

* *

"Thus ends the history of Jack Halyard, the Sailor Boy; which leads to important reflections on the affairs of the world, and the great objects of human pursuit. By his example, we learn how much depends on merit, and how little on the outward circumstances of fortune. . . . We see, by the fate of Carthage, how cities may prosper or decline, by the moral conduct of their people.

". . . In this free land, let the old teach the young, that all true glory consists in noble minds and glorious deed; and that there is no real greatness on earth, but the will and power of being greatly good."

from *The Story of Jack Halyard* by
William Cardell [pp. 149 and 150]

Notes

Notes to Introduction

1. Phillippe Aries, *Centuries of Childhood* (1962); John Demos, *A Little Commonwealth* (1970), especially the discussion in pp. 180-190; Bernard W. Wishey, *The Child and the Republic* (1968), especially the Preface, pp. vii-x, and pp. 3-5.

2. See William Sloane, *English and American Children's Books in the Seventeenth Century* (1955), and Monica Kiefer, *American Children through Their Books, 1700-1835* (1948).

3. These remarks refer to original American juvenile fiction, not to retellings or translations of other works, such as Hawthorne's *Wonder Book*.

4. This is true even of the least realistic, least didactic of fiction. Alice plainly represents those English qualities of character Charles Dodgson admired: self-possession, pleasant manners, and an unshakable independence of mind.

5. Russell B. Nye, *"History and Literature,"* in Robert Bremner, *ed., Essays on History and Literature* (Columbus: Ohio State University Press, 1966), p. 140.

6. See Frank Mott, *Golden Multitudes* (New York: Macmillan Co., 1947), p. 5.

7. See, for example, R. Richard Wohl, "The 'Rags to Riches Story,' " in Reinhart Bendix and Seymour M. Lipset, *Class, Status and Power* (1953), pp. 388-395; and Michael Zuckerman, "The Nursery Tales of Horatio Alger," *American Quarterly* 24 (May 1972): 191-209.

8. Hawthorne was the only exception, and his few fictional works for children, while somewhat better in style than other juvenile fiction, did not differ markedly from them in other respects.

9. See Cornelia Meigs et al., *A Critical History of Children's Literature,* rev. ed. (New York: Macmillan Co., 1969).

10. See Catherine Maria Sedgwick, *Home* (1838), p. 12. Lucy Larcom, in her autobiographical *A New England Girlhood* (1889), said that she was considered a child until her thirteenth birthday, when her hair was put up, her skirts let down, and she was henceforward counted an adult. See pp. 78, 166-167.

11. Alexis de Tocqueville, *Democracy in America* (1945 ed.), 2:192.

12. See Hellmut Lehmann-Haupt, *The Book in America* (1952), pp. 123-124; Albert Van Nostrand, *The Denatured Novel* (1956), p. 31; Mott, *Golden Multitudes,* pp. 7-9.

13. Larcom, *New England Girlhood*, p. 101; Edward Everett Hale, *A New England Boyhood* (1893), p. 81; William T. Venable, *A Buckeye Boyhood* (1911), p. 135. Dr. Heman Humphrey, president of Amherst College for twenty-two years and an ardent writer on child nurture, added further testimony when he complained that "this eager pouring over storybooks at so tender an age . . . retards the growth, and robs the little cheek of its fulness and its color." (Quoted in Anne L. Kuhn, *The Mother's Role in Childhood Education* [1947], p. 25.)

14. See Kiefer, *American Children through Their Books*. This attitude prevades her work, but see pp. 6, 22, 44, and 225, for example. Jacob Blanck, in "A Twentieth Century Look at Nineteenth Century Children's Books" in William Targ, *Bibliophile in the Nursery* (Cleveland: World Publishing Co., 1957), pp. 427-451, makes a similar assumption.

15. Jean Piaget, *The Child's Conception of Physical Causality* (Paterson, N.J.: Littlefield, Adams and Co., 1961), p. 281.

16. Richard Sennett, *The Uses of Disorder* (New York: Alfred A. Knopf, 1970), pp. 5-6.

Notes to Chapter I

1. Nathaniel Willis, Prospectus, *Youth's Companion*, 16 April 1827, p. 1.

2. Ibid.

3. William Cardell, *Jack Halyard* (1825), p. x. Cardell (1780-1828), teacher and author of an English grammar, wrote only two children's books, *Jack Halyard* and *The Happy Family*. Little more is known about him. He is quoted frequently in this study because he so often expressed explicitly views which were pervasive but tacit in most children's fiction of the period.

4. Ibid.

5. [Lydia Maria Child], *Evenings in New England*, p. iii. This collection of stories was published as "By an American Lady" in 1824, but later books by Mrs. Child list it among her works.

6. Hellmut Lehmann-Haupt, *The Book in America*, 2d ed. (1952), p. 123.

7. Samuel G. Goodrich, *Recollections of a Lifetime* (1856), 2:388-390.

8. Ibid., 1:174.

9. Edwin Rice, *The Sunday School Movement and the American Sunday School Union* (1917), pp. 146-147.

10. Ibid., pp. 141-144.

11. Carlton Bruce, *Pleasure and Profit* (1835), p. 44.

12. Rice, *Sunday School Movement*, p. 144.

13. Samuel G. Goodrich, *Parley's Book of Fables* (1836), p. 6.

14. Goodrich, *Recollections*, 2:320-321.

15. William Cardell, *The Happy Family* (1828), p. 10.

16. Goodrich, *Parley's Book of Fables*, p. 6.

17. Sara Parton [Fanny Fern], *The Play-Day Book* (1857), p. iv.

18. Willis, "Prospectus," *Youth's Companion*, 16 April 1827, p. 1.

19. Jacob Abbott, *Harper's Monthly Story Book* (1854), preface.

20. Catherine Beecher, *Treatise on Domestic Economy*, rev. ed. (1848), p. 36.

21. Catherine Maria Sedgwick, *Boy of Mt. Rhigi* (1848), pp. 5-7.

22. Cardell, *Jack Halyard*, p. xii.

23. Ibid., pp. xi, xii. Richard Hofstadter examines the long-range implications of this distinction between character and intellect in *Anti-Intellectualism in American Life* (New York: Alfred Knopf [Vintage Books], 1962), chapter 12 especially.

24. Ibid., p. ix.

25. *The Juvenile Miscelleny* (1826), 1:31.

26. *Sarah and Her Cousins* (1831), p. 11.

27. Lydia Sigourney, *The Girl's Book* (1837), p. 7.

28. Goodrich, *Recollections of a Lifetime*, 1:55. A very detailed statement of the family's responsibility for the moral character of children can be found in Horace Bushnell, *Christian Nurture* (1847), especially chapter 4.

29. Beecher, *Treatise on Domestic Economy*, p. 37.

30. Daniel Webster, "Influence of Woman," in Rufus W. Griswold, ed., *Prose Writers of America*, p. 185. The speech is an excellent summary of prevailing views toward mothers and education. For a thorough discussion of the role assigned to mothers in the period, see Anne L. Kuhn, *The Mother's Role in Childhood Education* (1947).

31. Maria McIntosh, excerpt printed in John Hart, *Female Prose Writers* (1852), pp. 72-73.

32. Quoted in Meade Minnigerode, *The Fabulous Forties, 1840-1850* (1924), p. 75.

33. William R. Taylor discusses Sarah J. Hale's career and outlook at length in *Cavalier and Yankee* (1961), pp. 115-141, pointing out the interplay between her representative experiences as an American and a woman in her era, and her attitudes toward family, children, women, and home.

34. On the scarcity of southern juvenile literature before 1860, see John C. Crandall, "Patriotism and Humantarian Reform in Children's Literature, 1825-1860," in *American Quarterly* 21 (Spring 1969): 18.

35. Whitney R. Cross, *The Burned Over District* (1950), p. 226.
36. *Juvenile Miscellany* 1 (1826): iii. Lydia Maria Child, *The Mother's Book* (1831), p. 80.
37. *Letters of Lydia Maria Child* (1883), p. 255.
38. Harriet Martineau, *The Martyr Age in America*, p. 216; quoted in Bernice G. Lamberton, "A Biography of Lydia Maria Child" (Ph. D. diss., University of Maryland, 1953), p. 66.
39. *Letters of L.M.C.*, Appendix, p. 264.
40. Lydia Maria Child, *An Appeal in Favor of That Class of Americans Called Africans* (New York: Arno Press, 1968), preface.
41. *Letters of L.M.C.*, pp. 16-17.
42. Ibid., Introduction, p. ix.
43. See John G. Whittier's "Biographical Introduction" in *Letters of L.M.C.*, pp. v-xxv.
44. Goodrich, *Recollections*, 2:321.
45. Jacob Abbott came closest, after Goodrich. His total output was even greater—180 titles—but some of these were adult books.
46. Goodrich, *Recollections*, 2:112.
47. Ibid., p. 543.
48. Ibid., 1:95.
49. Ibid., pp. 167, 169.
50. Ibid., 1:172; 2:167.
51. Ibid., 1:11.
52. E. Douglas Branch, *The Sentimental Years* (1934), pp. 307-308.
53. See Gordon Haight, *Mrs. Sigourney* (1930), *passim*.
54. Goodrich, *Recollections*, 2:333-334.
55. Ibid., p. 321.
56. Ibid.

Notes to Chapter II

1. William Cardell, *The Happy Family* (1828), p. 10. For similar statements, see *Self-Willed Susie* (1860), p. 150, and [W. Simonds] *Jessie* (1859), advertisement in front of book.
2. Jacob Abbott, *Franconia Tales: Malleville* (1850), p. vi.
3. In *Love Token* (1838), p. 69.
4. Cardell, *Jack Halyard* (1825), p. ix.
5. Eliza Follen, *The Well-Spent Hour* (1832), p. 76.

6. Phillippe Aries, *Centuries of Childhood* (1962), p. 32. See also Anne L. Kuhn, *The Mother's Role in Childhood Education* (1947), chapter 5.

7. E. Cornelius, *Little Osage Captive* (1832), p. viii.

8. *Juvenile Miscellany*, n.s. 3 (1830): 16.

9. *The Morton Family* (1845), p. 7.

10. Mrs. E. Sedgewick, *Moral Tales* (1845), p. 163.

11. *Two Little Orioles* (1859), pp. 8-9.

12. Jacob Abbott, *Franconia Tales: Wallace* (1850), title page.

13. [Lydia Maria Child], *Evenings in New England* (1824), p. 27.

14. Mrs. Sigourney lived in Hartford; Mrs. Follen, Frances Osgood (a contributor to *The Juvenile Miscellany*) and S. G. Goodrich in Boston; C. M. Sedgwick spent most winters in New York City.

15. Lydia Sigourney, *The Girl's Book* (1851), pp. 85-86.

16. *The Child's Portfolio* (1823), unpaged.

17. See, for example, Abbott, *Franconia Tales: Malleville* (1850); *Not Rich, But Generous* (1851), p. 151; Jacob Abbott, *Caleb in the Country* (1839); *Juvenile Miscellany* 1 (1826): 15.

18. See *The Haymakers* (1832), pp. 6-7; Aunt Friendly, *Bound Out* (1859), *passim*.

19. Quoted in James D. Hart, *The Popular Book* (1950), p. 91.

20. Maria McIntosh, *Ellen Leslie* (1842), p. 54.

21. *Juvenile Miscellany*, 3d ser., 5 (1833): 159.

22. Cardell, *Jack Halyard*, p. 23.

23. *Mary and Thomas* (1830), unpaged.

24. Aunt Friendly, *Bound Out* (1859), pp. 18, 20, 22.

25. Attitudes toward class, however, often help to identify stories; American authors generally assumed flexible class lines; English authors did not. Also, English authors were often more vivid writers than most Americans of the period. See Gillian Avery, *Nineteenth Century Children* (1965).

26. *Sarah and Her Cousins* (1831), p. 27.

27. Abbott, *Franconia Tales: Malleville*, p. v.

28. Cardell, *Jack Halyard*, p. viii.

29. *Not Rich, But Generous* (1851), p. 44.

30. Aunt Friendly, *Bound Out*, p. 89.

31. *Juvenile Miscellany* 2 (1827): 8.

32. Sigourney, *Girl's Book*, pp. 82, 85.

33. See, for example, "The Cousins" in *Youth's Companion*, May 7, 1846, p. 3, and May 13, 1846, p. 13.

34. Sigourney, *Girl's Book*, p. 123.

35. *The Contrast* (1832), pp. 18-19.

36. See *Belle and Lillie* (1857).

37. See *The Contrast*, pp. 33-60, and [Mrs. Harriet W. Baker]

"Faithful Hannah" and "Manovers" in *Howard and His Teacher* (1859).

38. See Justyn's story in "Mill-Hill," in C. M. Sedgwick, *Love Token* (1838), pp. 105-136.

39. *The Bud, the Flower and the Fruit* (1854), p. 17.

40. *Juvenile Miscellany,* 3d ser., 5 (1833): 168. The same warning in almost the same words was given in Mrs. F. H. McDougall, *The Envoy* (1840), p. 37.

41. John Demos, *A Little Commonwealth* (1970), chapter 4, demonstrates that the nuclear family was the norm for Plymouth Colony. Perhaps the extended family has always been as much myth as reality in the United States.

42. [Sedgwick, Susan], *The Children's Week* (1830), p. 4.

43. See, for instance, tales by C. M. Sedgwick, especially "Mill-Hill" in *Love Token,* and any of "Aunt Friendly's" stories.

44. Samuel G. Goodrich, *Parley's Book of Fables* (1836), p. 56.

45. Ibid., p. 15.

46. Cardell, *Jack Halyard,* p. 139.

47. *Father's Pictures of Family Influence* (1847), p. 11.

48. *The Contrast*, p. 10.

49. Ibid., p. 10.

50. Ibid., p. 18.

51. See Oneida Seaton, *It Is All for the Best* (1845); *The Child of Want and Misery* (1824); *The Cooper's Son* (1846), p. 11; Catherine Trowbridge, *Dick and His Friend Fidus* (1859), among many others. By the 1850s, there began to be exceptions to this general statement. See page 000.

52. Samuel G. Goodrich, *Peter Parley's Short Stories for Long Nights* (1834), pp. 11, 14.

53. Catherine Maria Sedgwick, *Stories for Young Persons* (1841), p. 16.

54. *Mary Wilson: A Tale of New England* (1846), p. 25.

55. David Rothman, *The Discovery of Asylum* (1971). See chapter 8 especially.

56. See *Laura's Impulses* (1854), pp. 88-89.

57. See page 000 ff.

58. *What Norman Saw in the West* (1859), pp. 18, 211.

59. See Robert Bremner, ed., *Children and Youth in America, 1600-1865,* 1 (1970): 759-760.

60. See Catherine Maria Sedgwick, *Stories for Young Persons* (1841), p. 75; *Social Visits* (1854), pp. 21, 22, 117; *The Child's Birthday* (1821), pp. 7, 9.

61. Mrs. Frances M. Cheseboro, *Smiles and Tears* (1858), pp. 98-104.

62. *Blind Susan* (1835), pp. 15-16.

63. *Nellie Russell* (1858), p. 39.

64. *The Country Schoolhouse* (1848), p. 27.
65. Abbott, *Franconia Tales: Mary Erskine* (1850), pp. 81-82.
66. *Adelaide* (1827), p. 22.
67. *A Juvenile Keepsake* (1851), p. 97.
68. Mrs. E. Sedgewick, *Moral Tales,* p. 86.
69. *The Bud, the Flower and the Fruit,* p. 44.
70. *The Morton Family* (1845), pp. 34, 49-50.
71. *Juvenile Miscellany,* 3d ser., 2 (1832): 52; C. M. Sedgwick, *Conquest and Self-Conquest* (1843), pp. 20-21; *Self-Willed Susie* (1860), p. 11.
72. For the general decline of fathers in the fiction, see pages 000 ff.
73. Goodrich, *Parley's Book of Fables,* pp. 119, 122.
74. Goodrich, *Peter Parley's Short Stories,* p. 14; *Alfred Raymond* (1854), p. 16; *Self-Willed Susie,* p. 150.

Notes to Chapter III

1. *Little Mary* (1831), by "A Mother," pp. 8-9, 15.
2. Ibid., p. 18.
3. Ibid., pp. 20, 30-36.
4. See Taylor, *Cavalier and Yankee,* p. 124.
5. Mrs. H. S. Grosvenor, *My Sister Emily* (1847), p. 71.
6. *Youth's Companion,* August 19, 1842, p. 60.
7. *Juvenile Miscellany* 1 (1826): 101.
8. Ibid., 3d ser., 2 (1832): 6.
9. Lydia Sigourney, *The Girl's Book* (1837), p. 44.
10. M. E. Bradley, *Douglass Farm* (1857), p. 99.
11. *Filial Duty Recommended and Enforced, by a Variety of Instructive and Amusing Narratives* (1847), p. [3].
12. Ibid., p. 37.
13. Eliza Follen, *Sequel to the Well-Spent Hour* (1832), p. 59.
14. *Childhood, or, Little Alice* (1855), p. 112.
15. Sigourney, *Girl's Book* (1837), p. 45.
16. *Filial Duty Recommended and Enforced* . . . , p. 4.
17. Sigourney, *Girl's Book,* pp. 45, 47.
18. Samuel G. Goodrich, *Parley's Book of Fables,* p. 43.
19. *The Country Schoolhouse* (1848), p. 27.

20. Goodrich, *Parley's Book of Fables*, pp. 17-18, 43.
21. Samuel G. Goodrich, *Peter Parley's Short Stories for Long Nights* (1834), pp. 35-36. Similar tales for young children were legion. See, for example, *The Child's Portfolio* (1823), unpaged; *The Girl's Own Book Full of Short Stories* (1831), unpaged; *Eight Stories for Isabel* (1832), pp. 4-5.
22. *Sarah and Her Cousins* (1831), p. 28.
23. Goodrich, *Peter Parley's Short Stories. . .* , pp. 76-79.
24. Ibid., p. 77. It is never explained in the story who it is who treats Edward as an inferior or forces him to do Edwin's will.
25. Ibid., p. 78.
26. Ibid., pp. 78-79.
27. Jacob Abbott, *Rollo at School* (1839), p. 92.
28. Ibid., p. 99.
29. Jacob Abbott, *The Rollo Philosophy* (1842), p. 79.
30. Ibid., pp. 85-86.
31. Jacob Abbott, *Franconia Tales: Mary Erskine* (1850), p. 22.
32. *Belle and Lilly* (1857), p. 30.
33. Aunt Friendly, *Bound Out* (1859), p. 61.
34. Grosvenor, *My Sister Emily*, pp. 26-29.
35. Clara Arnold, ed., *A Juvenile Keepsake* (1851), p. 110.
36. David J. Rothman, in chapter 4 of *The Discovery of the Asylum* (1971), discusses the "silent system" advocated during this period for rehabilitation of criminals.
37. *Juvenile Miscellany*, 3d ser., 2 (1832): 225.
38. Catherine M. Trowbridge, *Dick and His Friend Fidus* (1859), p. 26; also see *William Parker* (1836), pp. 16-17.
39. Eliza Leslie, *Stories for Adelaide* (1843), p. 98.
40. *Juvenile Miscellany*, n.s., 1 (1828): 132.
41. Amerel, *The Summer Holidays* (1850), p. 91. John Demos, *A Little Commonwealth* (1970), pp. 136-137, points out that recent studies suggest that Puritanism was more repressive toward anger and aggression than toward sex. Antebellum children's fiction's alarmed references to "the passions" also generally meant aggressive or at least antisocial feeling, not sexual emotion.
42. [Mrs. Harriet W. Baker], *Howard and His Teacher* (1859), p. 48
43. [Lydia Maria Child], *Evenings in New England,* p. 89.
44. Jacob Abbott, *Caleb in the Country* (1839), pp. 37-39.
45. Aunt Mary, *The Daisy* (1855), pp. 27-29.
46. *Youth's Companion,* 27 May 1842, p. 15.
47. *Ellen* (1821), p. 10.
48. Ibid., pp. 12, 15, 16.
49. *Juvenile Miscellany* 4 (1828): 76.
50. *Youth's Companion*, June 3, 1842, p. 16.

51. *Parley's Magazine* (1842), p. 272.
52. *Sarah and Her Cousins* (1831), p. 65.
53. Catherine M. Sedgwick, *Love Token* (1838), p. 98.
54. Catherine M. Sedgwick, *Boy of Mt. Rhigi* (1848), p. 139.
55. Carlton Bruce, *Pleasure and Profit* (1835), p. 195.
56. Ibid.
57. Sigourney, *Girl's Book* (1837), p. 8.
58. Louisa C. Tuthill, *Get Money* (1858), p. 247.
59. *Harry Winter, The Shipwrecked Sailor Boy* (1832), p. 5.
60. Sedgwick, *Love Token* (1838), pp. 34-39.
61. Cardell, *Happy Family*, p. 12.
62. Bruce, *Pleasure and Profit*, p. 13.
63. *Juvenile Keepsake* (1851), pp. 52-57.
64. Bruce, *Pleasure and Profit*, pp. 16, 185.
65. *Juvenile Miscellany* 2 (1827): 63.
66. See Monica Kiefer, *American Children through Their Books* (1948), chapter 2, for a sense of how long the literature for children (largely non-fictional and religious) retained the concept of evil in child nature. See also Anne L. Kuhn, *The Mother's Role in Childhood Education* (1947), pp. 53-54, for a discussion of Dr. Heman Humphrey, author of *Domestic Education* (1840), and the mix of conservatism and progressive thought in his views on child nurture.
67. *Self-Willed Susie*, p. 126. There are dozens of similar statements in the literature. See, for instance, Spencer Cone, *The Fairies in America* (1859), p. 6; Eliza Follen, *Twilight Stories* (1858), p. 31; *A Juvenile Keepsake* (1851), p. 23.
68. Horace Bushnell, *Christian Nurture* (1888; first published 1847). This was, in turn, close to the much older Quaker view of the inborn nature of children as *amoral*. See Kiefer, *American Children through Their Books*, chapter 2, p. 39.
69. *Laura's Impulses* (1854), p. 101.
70. *Alfred Raymond* (1854), p. 5.
71. C. M. Sedgwick, *Conquest and Self-Conquest* (1843), p. 55.
72. *The Cooper's Son* (1848), p. 12.

Notes to Chapter IV

1. Catherine Maria Sedgwick, *Love Token* (1838), p. 53.
2. *Mary Wilson: A Tale of New England* (1846), p. 13.
3. *The Contrast* (1832), p. 11.
4. *Sarah and Her Cousins* (1831), p. 72.
5. [Susan Sedgwick], *The Children's Week* (1830), p. 33.
6. *Juvenile Miscellany*, n. s. 4 (1830): 236.
7. Catherine Maria Sedgwick, *Boy of Mt. Rhigi* (1848), p. 181.
8. *Juvenile Miscellany*, 3d ser., 2 (1832): 165.
9. [Lydia Maria Child], *Evenings in New England* (1824), p. 41. William M. Thayer's *The Bobbin Boy* (1860) devoted several pages to a discussion of distinguished men who were backward scholars in their youth. See pp. 26-28.
10. Bray Hammond, "Jackson, Biddle and the Bank of the United States," *Journal of Economic History* 7 (May 1947): 23.
11. Eliza Leslie, *Birth Day Stories* (1840), p. 23.
12. See, for example, the struggles of Georgy's Aunt Amy in Mrs. O. A. S. Beale's *Georgy Lee* (1859), and Mary in *Mary Wilson* (1846).
13. See Arthur Calhoun, *A Social History of the American Family* (1918), vol. 2, chapter 9.
14. An exception to this general statement was Fanny Fern (Sara Parton), who often appeared in her own tales as narrator. See *Little Ferns for Fanny's Little Friends* (1854) and *The Play-Day Book* (1857).
15. Jacob Abbott, *Franconia Tales: Agnes* (1853), p. 214.
16. For a typical example in juvenile fiction, see Parton, *Play-Day Book*, pp. 256-257. For similar ideas expressed with more precision in writing for adults, see Fred Somkin, *Unquiet Eagle* (1967), pp. 16-17.
17. *The Bud, the Flower and the Fruit* (1854), p. 35.
18. *The Canal Boat* (1848), p. 27, 33.
19. [S. Sedgwick], *The Children's Week*, p. 29.
20. Leslie, *Birth Day Stories*, p. 8.
21. Ibid., pp. 21-23.
22. C. M. Sedgwick, *Love Token*, p. 92.
23. In *Not Rich, But Generous* (1851), pp. 11-25.
24. *Laura's Impulses* (1854), p. 84.
25. In *A Juvenile Keepsake* (1851), pp. 32-39.
26. Ibid., pp. 33-34.
27. *Laura's Impulses*, p. 41.
28. C. M. Sedgwick, *Love Token*, p. 26.
29. Ibid., p. 128.
30. Lydia Maria Child, *The Little Girl's Own Book* (1831), p. iii. This social mobility was a major theme of Catherine Maria Sedgwick's didactic novel of family life, *Home* (1835). See especially pp. 39 and 48.

31. *The Morton Family* (1845), pp. 22-23.
32. Miss L. Bancroft, "The Week's Probation," in *Juvenile Miscellany*, n. s. 6 (1831):184.
33. C. M. Sedgwick, *Love Token*, p. 81.
34. See Eliza Follen, *Sequel to the Well-Spent Hour* (1832), p. 41.
35. [Mrs. Harriet Baker], *Howard and His Teacher* (1859), p. 17; *Youth's Companion*, 13 November 1856, p. [117]. For other examples of representative attitudes toward the Irish, see *Morton Family*, pp. 22-23; *Juvenile Miscellany*, n.s. 3 (1830):230-238; *The Country Schoolhouse* (1848), pp. 41-42.
36. Aunt Julia, *The Temperance Boys* (1858), pp. 69-101.
37. *The Essays of Ralph Waldo Emerson*, The First Series and The Second Series (New York: Heritage Press, 1934), p. 248.
38. For the relationship between anti-war and anti-slavery sentiment, see Louis Filler, *The Crusade Against Slavery* (1960), especially pp. 33, 183-185; and Alice Tyler, *Freedom's Ferment* (1944), chapter 15, especially pp. 415-417.
39. *Charles Ashton, The Boy That Would Be a Soldier* (1823). p. 108 (hereafter cited as *Charles Ashton*).
40. Ibid., p. 107.
41. Joseph Alden, *The Old Revolutionary Soldier* (1848), p. 67.
42. *Charles Ashton*, pp. 91-95.
43. Ibid., p. 106.
44. Alden, *Old Revolutionary Soldier*, pp. 54-58.
45. *Charles Ashton,* p. 16.
46. Alden, *Old Revolutionary Soldier*, p. 123.
47. Ibid., pp. 52, 58-59.
48. *Charles Ashton*, p. [5].
49. Samuel G. Goodrich, *Peter Parley's Juvenile Tales* (1851), p. 49.
50. In Lydia Sigourney, *Olive Leaves* (1852), pp. 34-48.
51. *Juvenile Miscellany* 4 (1830):240.
52. Aunt Julia, *The Brandy Drops* (1858), pp. 70-71.
53. *Youth's Companion*, 19 August 1842, p. 63.
54. *The Haymakers* (1832), p. 7.
55. Aunt Julia, *The Brandy Drops*, pp. 15, 28.
56. Ibid., p. 68.
57. Ibid., pp. 86-87.
58. In *The Temperance Tales*, vol. 3 (1840).
59. Eliza Lee Follen, *Sequel to the Well-Spent Hour, or The Birthday* (1832), p. 82.
60. Eliza Lee Follen, *Twilight Tales: May Mornings and New Year's Eve* (1858), p. 15.
61. Ibid., p. 22.

62. Ibid., pp. 15-16.

63. [Lydia Maria Child], *Evenings in New England* (1824), pp. 138-147.

64. Mrs. Child's best-known books for children, *Flowers for Children* (3 vols., 1844, 1845, 1847), are compilations of some of her writing for the *Miscellany*.

65. See *Letters of Lydia Maria Child* (1883), p. 255.

66. *Juvenile Miscellany*, n.s. 4 (1830):88. For a very similar story for young children, see *Juvenile Miscellany*, 3d ser., 4 (1833):53.

67. *Juvenile Miscellany*, n.s. 3 (1832):47.

68. Ibid., 5 (1830):292.

69. Ibid., pp. 294-295.

70. Ibid., p. 299.

71. *Letters of L.M.C.,* Introduction, p. ix.

72. The demise of *The Juvenile Miscellany* is usually attributed to the publication of the *Appeal*, though Louis Filler, in *The Crusade Against Slavery* (p. 59), says that this document had only a small and local circulation. In any case, Mrs. Child's views were generally known, even if they did not appear often in the *Miscellany*, and it may be that the magazine suffered from the worsening climate of opinion toward abolitionists after 1833 more than from any one piece of writing by its editor.

73. The most famous example of these themes in adult literature is, of course, Harriet Beecher Stowe's *Uncle Tom's Cabin* (1852).

74. *Jemmy and His Mother* (1858), p. 39.

75. *Walter Browning* (1859), p. 22.

76. For the general caution of publishers on the subject of slavery, see Filler, *Crusade Against Slavery*, pp. 260-262. The ASSU and The American Tract Society were strongly attacked by abolitionists for their silence on the moral wrong of slavery.

77. See Catherine Maria Sedgwick, *Conquest and Self-Conquest* (1843), p. 135.

Notes to Chapter V

1. Sara Parton [Fanny Fern], *The Play Day Book* (1857), p. 8. The author was the daughter of Nathaniel Willis, editor of *The Youth's Companion*, and wife of James Parton, the historian.

2. William Cardell, *Jack Halyard* (1825), p. ix.

3. See R. Richard Wohl, "The 'Rags to Riches Story' " in Reinhard Bendix and Seymour Martin Lipset, eds., *Class, Status and Power* (1953), pp. 388-395. John G. Cawelti, *Apostles of the Self-Made Man* (1965), pp. 116-118, makes the same point.

4. *Alfred Raymond* (1859). Again, there are clear parallels with the Alger tales. See Wohl, "Rags to Riches," p. 390.

5. William Taylor Adams [Oliver Optic], *Poor and Proud* (1854), p. 18.

6. *Alfred Raymond*, pp. 16, 27.

7. *Laura's Impulses* (1854), p. 89.

8. Ibid., p. 88.

9. *The Canal Boat* (1848), p. 17.

10. Catherine Maria Sedgwick, *Love Token* (1838), pp. 134-135.

11. Maria McIntosh, *Ellen Leslie* (1842), p. 51.

12. *Sloth and Thrift* (1847), p. 6. Carroll Rosenburg finds this shift in attitude taking place within the New York charitable societies about ten years earlier than it appears with any frequency in children's books. Much of it she ascribes to the panic of 1837, which multiplied the problems of poverty and need drastically. See Rosenburg, *Religion and the Rise of the American City* (1971), pp. 156-158.

13. T. S. Arthur, *Maggy's Baby* (1852), p. 36. For a discussion of the development of institutional care of the poor in this period, see David J. Rothman, *The Discovery of the Asylum* (1971), especially chapters 7 and 8.

14. *The Child's Portfolio* (1823), unpaged. For other examples of early attitudes, see also Lydia Maria Child, *The Little Girl's Own Book* (1831), [p. 4]; *The Child of Want and Misery* (1824), unpaged; *Tales for Thomas* (1830), pp. 10-11.

15. *Laura's Impulses*, p. 93.

16. Adams, *Poor and Proud*, pp. 29, 33, 34.

17. Ibid., pp. 33, 80, 163.

18. Louisa C. Tuthill, *Get Money* (1858), pp. 114, 125.

19. Adams, *Poor and Proud,* p. 140.

20. *Belle and Lilly* (1857), p. 29.

21. [Mrs. Harriet Baker], *Howard and His Sister* (1859), pp. 22, 97.

22. Tuthill, *Get Money,* p. 29.

23. See Anne Abbott's tale, *The Olneys* (1846). Paternal mismanagement was a fault often noted by foreign visitors, according to Arthur Calhoun, *A Social History of the American Family* (1918), vol. 2, p. 131.

24. For a perceptive discussion of the feminine hostilities expressed through the domestic novels of the period, see Helen Papashivly, *All the Happy Endings* (1956).

25. Mrs. O. A. S. Beale, *Georgy Lee* (1859), pp. 80-81.

26. Ibid., pp. 85, 91, 106.

27. Ibid., pp. 123, 129.

28. Michael Zuckerman, in "The Nursery Tales of Horatio Alger," *American Quarterly* 24, no. 2 (May 1972): 191-299, points out that Alger's heroes aspired only to the level of respectability. But William M. Thayer's *Bobbin Boy* (1860), often considered an Alger-like hero, "was known to fame as His Excellency, The Governor of _____" (p. 308).

29. *The Youth's Companion*, 7 April 1854, pp. 1-2.

30. *The Cooper's Son* (1846), p. 65.

31. Anne Abbott, *The Olneys*, p. 16.

32. Tuthill, *Get Money*, pp. 67-68, 78.

33. Beale, *Georgy Lee*, pp. 60-61.

34. Ibid., p. 70

35. John S. C. Abbott, *The Mother at Home*, 2d ed. (Boston: Crocker and Brewster, 1833), p. 149.

36. *Youth's Companion*, 20 December 1855, p. 140.

37. Sara Parton [Fanny Fern], *Little Ferns for Fanny's Little Friends* (1854), p. 48.

38. See *Alfred Raymond*.

39. See Parton, *Little Ferns . . .* , pp. 33-35, 118.

40. See Cawelti, *Apostles of the Self-Made Man*, pp. 4-5.

Notes to Chapter VI

1. The basic source for the description of economic growth is C. Douglas North, *The Economic Growth of the United States, 1790-1860* (1966). Statistics are from George Taylor, *The Transportation Revolution, 1815-1860*, vol. 4 of *The Economic History of the United States* (1951).

2. Marvin Meyers, *The Jacksonian Persuasion* (1957), p. 4.

3. Leonard White, *The Jacksonians* (1954), surveys the political changes of the Jacksonian era.

4. Edward Everett Hale, *A New England Boyhood* (1893), pp. xii, xiii.

5. Alice Tyler, *Freedom's Ferment* (1944), surveys many of the era's enthusiasms and reform movements.

6. See Fred Somkin, *Unquiet Eagle* (1967), chapter 1, for a sampling of the standard rhetoric of the time.

7. Meyers, *The Jacksonian Persuasion*, p. 7. William R. Taylor, *Cavalier and Yankee* (1961), and Fred Somkin, *Unquiet Eagle* (1967), also examine the ambivalent American response to change in this period.

8. See Margaret Mead, Address presented to the Midcentury White House Conference on Children and Youth, Washington, D. C., 1950; and Kenneth Keniston, *The Uncommitted: Alienated Youth in American Society* (New York: Harcourt, Brace and World, 1960).

9. Alexis de Tocqueville, *Democracy in America* (1945), vol. 2, p. 99.

10. Quoted in William E. Bridges, "Warm Hearth, Cold World," *American Quarterly* 21 (Winter 1969): 773.

11. Tocqueville, *Democracy in America*, vol. 2, pp. 192-193.

12. Arthur W. Calhoun, *A Social History of the American Family* (1918), vol. 2, p. 11.

13. Calhoun, *Social History*, vol. 2, pp. 51-70, quotes many such comments by foreign visitors. Even Harriet Martineau, whose remarks were characteristically friendly on the subject, emphasized the "independence and fearlessness" of American children. See *Society in America* (1837), vol. 2, p. 271. See also Richard L. Rapson, "The American Child as Seen by British Travellers, 1845-1935," *American Quarterly* 24 (Fall 1965): 520-34.

14. *Juvenile Miscellany*, 3d ser., 2 (1837): 7.

15. Samuel G. Goodrich, *Parley's Book of Fables* (1836), p. 53.

16. *Filial Duty Recommended and Enforced* . . . , p. 4.

17. Tocqueville himself, though he distinguished individualism from selfishness, predicted that unrestrained individualism might be "absorbed in downright selfishness" (*Democracy in America*, vol. 2, p. 98).

18. *Belle and Lilly* (1857), p. 30.

19. For a discussion of these reform ideas, see Anne L. Kuhn, *The Mother's Role in Childhood Education* (1947), chapter 3.

20. Eliza Follen, *Sequel to the WellSpent Hour* (1832), p. 32.

21. Catherine Maria Sedgwick, *Love Token* (1838), p. 121.

22. See David J. Rothman, *The Discovery of the Asylum* (1971), chapter 9.

23. *Sloth and Thrift* (1847), pp. 6-7.

24. Maria McIntosh, *Ellen Leslie* (1842), pp. 15, 18.

25. For discussions of this conflict in the period, see David Brion Davis, *Homicide in American Fiction, 1798-1860* (1957), and Carroll Rosenberg, *Religion and the Rise of the American City: The New York City Mission Movement, 1812-1870* (1971), pp. 267-268.

26. Harriet Beecher Stowe, "Uncle Abel and Little Edward," *Youth's Companion*, 3 April 1845, p. 190.

27. William Cardell, *Jack Halyard* (1825), p. xi.

28. Quoted in Herbert Ross Brown, *The Sentimental Novel in America, 1789-1860* (1940), p. 358.

29. William Dean Howells, *A Boy's Town* (New York: Harper Bros., 1890), p. 14.

30. Carlton Bruce, *Pleasure and Profit* (1835), p. 13.

31. Catherine Maria Sedgwick, *Boy of Mt. Rhigi* (1848), p. 221.

32. Horace Bushnell, *Christian Nurture* (1847), p. 15.

33. Ibid.

34. Clara Arnold, ed., *A Juvenile Keepsake* (1851), p. 57.

35. *Parley's Magazine*, May 1842, pp. 299-300.

36. D. H. Lawrence, *Studies in Classic American Literature* (1923), p. 160.

37. Nathaniel Hawthorne, *House of the Seven Gables* (Boston: Ticknor, Reed and Fields, 1851), p. 296.

Selected Bibliography

I. PRIMARY SOURCES—CHILDREN

Abbott, Anne W. *The Lost Wheelbarrow*. Boston: S. G. Simpkins, 1846.

————. *The Olneys*. Boston: James Munroe & Co., 1846.

Abbott, Jacob. *Caleb in the Country*. Boston: Crocker & Brewster, 1839.

————. *Cousin Lucy on the Sea Shore*. Boston: B. B. Mussey, 1844.

————. *Franconia Tales*. 10 vols. New York: Harper & Bros., 1850-1853.

————. *The Great Elm*. New York: Harper & Bros., [1854].

————. *Harper's Story Books*. Vol. 1. New York: Harper & Bros., 1854.

————. *Jonas on a Farm in Winter*. Boston: W. D. Ticknor, 1842.

————. *Rollo at School*. Boston: T. H. Carter, 1839.

————. *The Rollo Philosophy*. Philadelphia: Hogan & Thompson, 1842.

Adams, M. H., ed. *The Rainbow and Other Stories*. Boston: James M. Usher, 1850.

Adams, William Taylor [Oliver Optic]. *All Aboard; or, Life on the Lake*. New York: Hurst & Co., 1855.

————. *Poor and Proud*. New York: Mershon Co., [1858].

Addie's Party. Boston: Andrew F. Graves, [1860?].

Adelaide; or, The Rainy Evening. Boston: Christian Register Office, 1827.

Alden, Joseph. *An Old Revolutionary Soldier*. New York: Gates & Stedman, 1848.

————. *The Cardinal Flower and Other Tales*. Boston: Benjamin Perlans & Co., 1845.

————. *The State Prisoner.* New York: Lane and Tippett, 1848.

Alfred Raymond; or, A Mother's Influence. Philadelphia: A.S.S.U., [1854].

Am I a Sinner? Philadelphia: A.S.S.U., 1850.

Amerel. *The Summer Holidays: A Story for Children.* New York: D. Appleton & Co., 1850.

The Amethyst; or, The Pleasures of Country Life. New York: Josiah Adams, 1847.

Annette Warington. Boston: Benjamin H. Greene, 1832.

Arthur, T. S. *Maggy's Baby and Other Stories.* Philadelphia: Lippincott, Grambo & Co., 1852.

Aunt Friendly. *Bound Out.* New York: Anson D. F. Randolph, 1859.

————. Poor Little Joe. New York: Anson D. F. Randolph, 1860.

Aunt Julia. *The Brandy Drops: A Temperance Story.* New York: Carlton & Porter, A.S.S.U., 1858.

————. *The Temperance Boys.* New York: Phillips & Hunt, 1858.

Aunt Mary. *The Daisy.* New York: Sheldon, Lamport & Blakeman, 1855.

[Baker, Caroline H.?] *Little Emma and Her Father; or, The Effects of Pride.* Philadelphia: Morgan and Yeager, [1820].

[Baker, Mrs. Harriet N.] *Howard and His Teacher, The Sister's Influence and Other Stories.* Boston: Shepard, Clark & Brown, 1859.

Baldwin, Edward. *Fables in Prose.* New Haven: Sidney's Press, 1824.

The Basket Makers. Philadelphia: A.S.S.U., 1825.

Beale, Mrs. O. A. S. *Georgy Lee.* New York: Carleton & Porter, A.S.S.U., 1859.

Belle and Lilly. [By "A New Pen."] Boston: Crosby, Nichols & Co., 1857.

Bennett, Mrs. Mary E. *The Cottage Girl; or, An Account of Ann Edwards.* Philadelphia: Sunday and Adult School Union, 1824.

Bessie Duncan. Philadelphia: S.S.U., 1858.

Book of Fables for the Amusement and Instruction of Children. Hartford: Oliver D. Cooke, 1820.

Boy's Own Book of Amusement and Instruction. Providence: Cory & Daniels, 1835.

Bradley, M. E. *Douglass Farm, A Juvenile Story.* New York: D. Appleton & Co., 1857.

Bruce, Carlton. *Pleasure and Profit; or, The Boy's Friend.* Vol. 2. Revised by Uncle Arthur. New York: Taylor & Gould, 1835.

The Bud, the Flower and the Fruit; or, The Effects of Education. [By "A Lady of Boston."] Boston: James Munroe & Co., 1854.

Caddell, Cecilia. *Blind Agnese.* New York: E. Dunigan & Bro., 1855.

The Canal Boat. Philadelphia: A.S.S.U., 1848.

Cardell, William Samuel. *The Happy Family.* 2d ed. Philadelphia: T. T. Ash, 1828.

————. *Story of Jack Halyard.* 3d ed. Philadelphia: Uriah Hunt, 1825.

Charles Ashton, the Boy That Would Be a Soldier. Boston: N. S. and J. Simkins, 1823.

Cheseboro, Mrs. Frances M. *Smiles and Tears.* Boston: Whittemore, Niles & Hall, 1858.

[Child, Lydia Maria.] *Evenings in New England.* Boston: Cummings, Hilliard & Co., 1824.

[Child, Lydia Maria.] *Emily Parker.* Boston: Bowles & Dearborn, 1827.

Child, Lydia Maria. *Flowers for Children.* 3 vols. New York: C. S. Francis & Co., 1844, 1845, 1847.

————. *The Little Girl's Own Book.* Boston: Carter, Hendee & Babcock, 1831.

Child, Lydia Maria, ed. *Rainbows for Children.* New York: C. S. Francis & Co., 1848.

The Child of Want and Misery. New York: S. King, 1824.

Childhood; or, Little Alice. New York: Carleton & Phillips, S.S.U., 1855.

The Child's Birthday. Boston: Samuel T. Armstrong and

Crocker & Brewster, 1821.

The Child's Own Story Book. New Haven: S. Babcock, 1825.

The Child's Portfolio. New York: Mahlon Day, 1823.

Clara Douglas; or, The Unrequited Love of a Mother. Philadelphia: A.S.S.U., 1855.

Cone, Spencer. *The Fairies in America.* New York: Pudney & Russell, 1859.

The Contrast. Boston: Cottons & Barnard, 1832.

The Cooper's Son. Boston: James French, 1846.

Cornelius, E. *Little Osage Captive.* Boston: Sabbath School Society, 1832.

The Country Schoolhouse. Philadelphia: A.S.S.U., 1848.

Durang, Mrs. Mary. *The Boys True Joy.* Philadelphia and New York: Fisher & Brother, 1847.

Eight Stones for Isabel. Concord: J. W. Moore & Co., 1832.

Ellen: A Tale in Three Parts. [By "An American Lady."] Boston: Samuel Armstrong and Crocker & Brewster, 1821.

Fanny and Emma. Philadelphia: A.S.S.U., 1855.

Father's Pictures of Family Influence for His Own Children. Holliston, Mass.: David Heard, Jr., 1847.

Filial Duty Recommended and Enforced. New York: O. Scott (for the Wesleyan Methodist Convention of America), 1847.

Follen, Eliza Lee. *Made-Up Stories.* Boston: Whittemore, Niles & Hall, 1856.

————. *The Well-Spent Hour.* 3d ed. Boston: Carter & Hendee, 1832.

————. *Sequel to The Well-Spent Hour.* Boston: Carter & Hendee, 1832.

————. *Twilight Stories.* 12 vols. Boston: Whittemore, Niles & Hall, 1858.

The Glass of Whiskey. Philadelphia: A.S.S.U., [1825].

The Good Boy. Wendell, Mass.: John Metcalf, [1832].

Goodrich, Samuel G. [Peter Parley]. *Cheerful Cherry.* London: Darton & Co., n.d.

————. *Parley's Book of Fables.* Hartford: White, Dwier & Co., 1836.

————. *Peter Parley's Juvenile Tales.* Rev. ed. Cincinnati:

Applegate & Co., 1851.

————. *Peter Parley's Little Leaves for Little Readers*. Boston: James Munroe & Co., 1844.

————. *Peter Parley's New Keepsake*. Cincinnati: Mack R. Barnitz, 1857.

————. *Peter Parley's Short Stories for Long Nights*. Boston: Allen & Ticknor, 1834.

Grosvenor, H. S. *My Sister Emily*. Boston: Sabbath School Society, 1847.

H., A. C., of Newport, R.I. *Tales for Thomas*. New York: Mahlon Day, 1830.

Harry. New York: Sold by J. B. Jansen, 1823.

Harry Winter, The Shipwrecked Sailor Boy. New York: Mahlon Day, 1832.

The Haymakers. Philadelphia: A.S.S.U., 1832.

James Somers, the Pilgrim's Son. [By "A Lady of New Haven."] New Haven: A. H. Maltby, 1827.

Jane Scott. Philadelphia: A.S.S.U., 1832.

Jemmy and His Mother; A Tale for Children. Cincinnati: American Reform Tract and Book Society, 1858.

A Juvenile Keepsake; A Gift Book for Young People. Edited by Clara Arnold. Boston: Phillips, Sampson & Co., 1851.

The Juvenile Miscellany. (Whole series: o.s., vols. 1-4; n.s., vols. 1-6; 3d ser., vols. 1-6.) Lydia Maria Child, ed. Boston: John Putnam, 1826-1834.

Laura's Impulses. Philadelphia: A.S.S.U., 1854.

Leslie, Eliza. *Birth Day Stories*. Philadelphia: Henry F. Anners, 1840.

————. *Stories for Adelaide*. Philadelphia: Henry F. Anners, 1843.

Little Mary. A Story for Children from Four to Five Years Old. [By "A Mother."] Boston: Cottons & Barnard, 1831.

M. of Lowell. *Blind Susan*. New York: Mahlon Day, 1835.

Mary and Thomas. New Haven: S. Babcock, 1830.

Mary Wilson: A Tale of New England. Boston: Waite, Peirce & Co., 1846.

McDougall, Mrs. F. H. *The Envoy: From Free Hearts to the*

Free. n.p.: The Juvenile Emancipation Society, 1840.

McIntosh, Maria J. *Ellen Leslie.* New York: Dayton & Newman, 1842.

The Morton Family. [By "A Young Lady."] Boston: James Munroe & Co., 1845.

Nellie Russell. New York: Carlton & Porter, S.S.U., 1858.

Not Rich, But Generous. Boston: James Usher, 1851.

Original Moral Tales Intended for Children and Young Persons. Boston: Bowles & Dearborn, 1828.

Parton, Sara [Fanny Fern]. *Little Ferns for Fanny's Little Friends.* Auburn, N.Y.: Derby & Miller, 1854.

_____. *The Play-Day Book.* New York: Mason Bros., 1857.

The Pearl; Affection's Gift. A Christmas and New Year's Present. Philadelphia: Thomas T. Ash, 1830.

Sarah and Her Cousins; or, Goodness Better Than Knowledge. Boston: Carter, Hendee & Babcock, 1831.

Seaton, Oneida. *It Is All for the Best.* Boston: William Ticknor & Co., 1845.

Sedgewick, Mrs. E. *Moral Tales for Young People.* Boston: Crosby and Nichols, 1845.

[Sedgwick, Ann L.] *The Children's Week.* Boston: Carter & Hendee, 1830.

Segwick, Catherine Maria. *Boy of Mt. Rhigi.* Boston: Charles H. Peirce, 1848.

_____. *Conquest and Self-Conquest.* New York: Harper & Bros., 1843.

_____. *A Love Token for Children.* New York: Harper & Bros., 1838.

_____. *Stories for Young Persons.* New York: Harper & Bros., 1841.

Self-Willed Susie and Her Sister Lena. New York: Carlton & Porter, S.S.U., 1860.

Sigourney, Lydia. *The Girl's Book.* New York: R. Carter & Bros., 1851.

_____. *Olive Leaves.* New York: R. Carter & Bros., 1852.

Simonds, W. [Walter Aimwell]. *Jessie.* Boston: Gould and Lincoln, 1859.

Sloth and Thrift. Philadelphia: A.S.S.U., [1847].

Smith, Mrs. E. Oakes. *Stories for Good Children*. Buffalo: George H. Derby & Co., 1851.

The Snow Drops; A Story for Good Little Girls. New Haven: S. Babcock, 1831.

The String of Pearls for Little Children. Boston: Massachusetts Sabbath School Society, 1847.

The Temperance Tales. Vol. 3 An Irish Heart, Well Enough for the Vulgar. Boston: Whipple & Damrell, 1840.

Thayer, William M. *The Bobbin Boy*. Boston: J. E. Tilton & Co., 1860.

—————. *The Happy New Year*. Boston: Cyrus Stone, 1853.

—————. *Merry Christmas*. Boston: Stone & Halpine, 1854.

The Trials of a School Girl. Boston: Leonard C. Bowles, 1832.

Trowbridge, C. M. *Dick and His Friend Fidus*. Philadelphia: William and Alfred Martien, 1859.

Tuthill, Mrs. Louisa C. *Anything for Sport*. Boston: William Crosby & H. P. Nichols, 1846.

—————. *Braggadocio; A Book for Boys and Girls*. New York: Chas. Scribner, 1851.

—————. *Edith, the Backwoods Girl*. New York: Chas. Scribner, 1859.

—————. *Get Money*. New York: Chas. Scribner, 1858.

The Two Little Girls. Philadelphia: A.S.S.U., 1859.

Uncle Charles. *Social Visits; or, A Few Chestnuts for the Children*. Charleston, S.C.: Southern Baptist Pub. Society, 1854.

Walter Browning; or, The Slave's Protector. Cincinnati: American Reform Tract and Book Society, 1859.

What Norman Saw in the West. New York: Carlton & Porter, S.S.U., 1859.

Whig Against Tory: A Tale of the Revolution for Children. New Haven: A. H. Maltby, 1831.

Whitaker, Mary Ann. *Alice's Dream*. Boston: Walker, Wise & Co., 1859.

William Parker. Northampton, Mass.: J. H. Butler, 1836.

Youth's Companion. Weekly publication, 1827-1860. New

York: Nathaniel Willis, publisher and editor.
Youth's Keepsake; A Christmas and New Year's Gift for Young People. Boston: Carter and Hendee, 1831.

II. PRIMARY SOURCES—ADULT:

Beecher, Catherine E. *A Treatise on Domestic Economy for the Use of Young Ladies at Home and at School.* Rev. ed. New York: Harper & Bros., 1848.
Bushnell, Horace. *Christian Nurture.* New Haven: Yale University Press, 1947.
Chevalier, Michael. *Society, Manners and Politics in the United States.* Boston: Weeks, Jordan & Co., 1839.
————. Child, Lydia Maria. *The Frugal Housewife.* Boston: March and Capen, 1829. *The Mother's Book.* Boston: Carter, Hendee and Babcock, 1831.
Goodrich, Samuel G. *Recollections of a Lifetime.* 2 vols. New York and Auburn: Miller, Orton & Mulligan, 1856.
Griswold, Rufus Wilmot. *Prose Writers of America.* Philadelphia: Porter and Coates, 1847; rev. ed. 1870.
Hale, Edward Everett. *A New England Boyhood.* New York: Cassell Publishing Co., 1893.
Hart, John S. *Female Prose Writers of America.* Philadelphia: E. H. Butler & Co., 1852.
Hoar, George F. *Autobiography of Seventy Years.* New York; Chas. Scribner's Sons, 1903.
Larcom, Lucy. *A New England Girlhood.* Boston and New York: Houghton Mifflin Co., 1889.
Letters of Lydia Maria Child. [Biographical introduction by John G. Whittier; appendix by Wendell Phillips.] Boston: Houghton Mifflin Co., 1883.
Marryat, Frederick. *Diary in America.* Edited by Jules Zanger. Bloomington, Ind.: Indiana University Press, 1960.

Martineau, Harriet. *Society in America.* 2 vols. New York: Saunders & Otley, 1837.

Sedgwick, Catherine Maria. *Home.* 15th ed. Boston: James Munroe & Co., 1839.

Tocqueville, Alexis de. *Democracy in America.* Edited by Phillips Bradley. 2 vols. New York: Alfred A. Knopf, 1945.

Trollope, Frances. *Domestic Manners of the Americans.* Edited by Donald Smalley. New York: Alfred A. Knopf, 1949.

Venable, William Taylor. *A Buckeye Boyhood.* Cincinnati: Robert Clarke Co., 1911.

III. SECONDARY SOURCES:

Addison, Daniel D. *Lucy Larcom.* Cambridge, Mass.: Riverside Press, 1894.

Aries, Philippe. *Centuries of Childhood: A Social History of Family Life.* Translated by Robert Baldick. New York: Alfred A. Knopf, 1962.

Avery, Gillian. *Nineteenth Century Children.* London: Hodder & Stoughton, 1965.

Barnes, Gilbert H. *The Anti-Slavery Impulse, 1830-1844.* New York: Appleton-Century, 1933.

Bode, Carl, ed. *American Life in the 1840s.* New York: Doubleday & Co., 1967.

Boorstin, Daniel. *The Americans: The National Experience.* New York: Random House, [1965].

Branch, E. D. *The Sentimental Years, 1836-1860.* New York: Appleton-Century, 1934.

Bremner, Robert H., ed. *Children and Youth in America.* Vol. 1. 1600-1865. Cambridge, Mass.: Harvard University Press, 1970.

Bridges, William E. "Warm Hearth, Cold World." *American Quarterly* 21 (Winter 1969):773-79.

Brown, Herbert Ross. *The Sentimental Novel in America, 1789-1860*. Durham, N.C.: Duke University Press, 1940.

Brown, Marianna. *The Sunday School Movement in America*. New York: F. Revell Co., 1901.

Calhoun, Arthur W. *A Social History of the American Family*. Vol. 2. From Independence through the Civil War. Cleveland: Arthur H. Clark Co., 1918.

Cawelti, John G. *Apostles of the Self-Made Man*. Chicago: University of Chicago Press, 1965.

Cowie, Alexander. "The Vogue of the Domestic Novel, 1850-70." *Southern Atlantic Quarterly* 41 (October 1942): 416-32.

Crandall, John C. "Patriotism and Humanitarian Reform in Children's Literature, 1825-1860." *American Quarterly* 21 (Spring 1969): 3-23.

Cross, Whitney R. *Burned Over District*. Ithaca, N.Y.: Cornell University Press, 1950.

Dahl, Curtis. "The American School of Catastrophe." *American Quarterly* 11 (Fall 1959):380-90.

Davis, David B. *Homocide in American Fiction, 1798-1860*. Ithaca, N.Y.: Cornell University Press, 1957.

DeMause, Lloyd, ed. *The History of Childhood*. New York: Psychohistory Press, 1974.

Demos, John. *A Little Commonwealth: Family Life in Plymouth Colony*. New York: Oxford University Press, 1970.

Donald, David H. *Lincoln Reconsidered*. New York: Alfred A. Knopf, 1956.

Duberman, Martin. *The Anti-Slavery Vanguard*. Princeton, N.Y.: Princeton University Press, 1965.

Ekirch, Arthur A. *The Idea of Progress in America, 1815-1860*. New York: AMS Press, [1969].

Elson, Ruth M. *Guardians of Tradition: American Schoolbooks of the Nineteenth Century*. Lincoln, Neb.: University of Nebraska Press, 1964.

Erikson, Erik H. *Childhood and Society*. Rev. ed. New York: Norton & Co., 1963.

Fiedler, Leslie A. *Love and Death in the American Novel*. Rev.

ed. New York: Stein & Day, 1966.

Filler, Louis. *The Crusade Against Slavery, 1830-1860*. New York: Harper & Bros., 1960.

Gabriel, Ralph H. *The Course of American Democratic Thought*. New York: Ronald Press, 1940.

Garland, Hamlin, *Boy Life on the Prairie* (1899; reprint ed., Lincoln, Neb.: University of Nebraska Press, 1961).

Goodsell, Willystine. *A History of the Family as a Social and Educational Institution*. New York: Macmillan Co., 1915.

Gordon, Michael, ed. *The American Family in Social-Historical Perspective*. New York: St. Martin's Press, 1973.

Griffin, Clifford S. *Their Brother's Keepers; Moral Stewardship in the United States, 1800-1865*. New Brunswick, N.J.: Rutgers University Press, [1960].

Haight, Gordon. *Mrs. Sigourney, The Sweet Singer of Hartford*. New Haven: Yale University Press, 1930.

Halsey, Rosalie V. *Forgotten Books of the American Nursery*. Boston: Charles E. Goodspeed & Co., 1911.

Hareven, Tamara, ed. *Anonymous Americans*. Englewood Cliffs, N.J.: Prentice-Hall, 1971.

Haroutunian, Joseph. *Piety Versus Moralism; The Passing of the New England Theology*. New York: Henry Holt, 1932. Reprinted Hamden, Conn.: Archon Books, 1964.

Hart, J. D. *The Popular Book*. New York: Oxford University Press, 1950.

Hunt, David. *Parents and Children in History*. New York: Basic Books, 1970.

Jeffrey, Kirk. "The Family as Utopian Retreat from the City: 19th Century." Soundings 55 (1972): 21-41.

Katz, Michael. *The Irony of American School Reform*. Cambridge, Mass.: Harvard University Press, 1968.

Kern, Stephen. "Psychodynamics of the Victorian Family." *History of Childhood Quarterly* 1 (1974): 437-462.

Kiefer, Monica. *American Children through Their Books*. Philadelphia: University of Pennsylvania Press, 1948.

Kraditor, Aileen. *Means and Ends in American Abolition*. [New York]: Pantheon Books, [1969].

Kuhn, Anne L. *The Mother's Role in Childhood Education: New England Concepts, 1830-1860.* New Haven: Yale University Press, 1947.

Lamberton, Berenice G. "A Biography of Lydia Maria Child." Ph. D. dissertation, University of Maryland, 1958.

Lawrence, D. H. *Studies in Classic American Literature.* New York: Viking Press, 1964.

Lehmann-Haupt, Hellmut. *The Book in America.* 2d ed. New York: R. R. Bowker Co., 1952.

Lewis, R. W. B. *The American Adam: Innocence, Tragedy and Tradition in the Nineteenth Century.* Chicago: University of Chicago Press, 1955.

McClusky, Neil. *Public Schools and Moral Education.* New York: Columbia University Press, 1958.

Mennel, Robert M. *Thorns and Thistles.* Hanover, N. H. : University Press of New England, 1973.

Meyers, Marvin. *The Jacksonian Persuasion.* Stanford, Calif.: Stanford University Press, 1957.

Miller, Perry. *The Life of the Mind in America, from the Revolution to the Civil War.* New York: Harcourt, Brace & World, [1965].

————. *Nature's Nation.* Cambridge, Mass.: Harvard University Press, 1967.

Minnigerode, Meade. *The Fabulous Forties, 1840-1850.* New York: G. P. Putnam's Sons, 1924.

Mosier, Richard D. *Making the American Mind.* New York: King's Crown Press, 1947.

Nash, Roderick. *Wilderness and the American Mind.* New Haven: Yale University Press, 1967.

North, Douglass C. *The Economic Growth of the United States, 1790-1860.* New York: W. W. Norton & Co., 1966.

Papashivly, Helen W. *All the Happy Endings.* New York: Harper & Bros., 1956.

Parrington, Vernon. *Main Currents in American Thought.* Vol. 2. The Romantic Revolution, 1800-1860. [New York: Harcourt, Brace & Co., 1927-30.]

Pattee, F. L. *The Feminine Fifties.* Port Washington, N.Y.: Kennikat Press, 1966.

Pessen, Edward. *Jacksonian America: Society, Personality and Politics*. Homewood, Ill.: Dorsey Press, 1969.

Pierson, G. W. *Tocqueville and Beaumont in America*. New York: Oxford University Press, 1938.

Potter, David M. *People of Plenty*. Chicago: University of Chicago Press, 1954.

Rabb, Theodore K. and Rotberg, Robert I. *The Family in History*. New York: Harper-Row, 1973.

Rapson, Richard L. "The American Child as Seen by British Travellers, 1845-1935." *American Quarterly* 27 (Fall 1965) 520-34.

Rice, Edwin W. *The Sunday School Movement and the American Sunday School Union*. Philadelphia, 1917.

Rosenberg, Carroll. *Religion and the Rise of the American City: The New York City Mission Movement, 1812-1870*. Ithaca, N.Y.: Cornell University Press, 1971.

Rothman, David. *The Discovery of the Asylum; Social Order and Disorder in the New Republic*. Boston: Little, Brown & Co., 1971.

Rourke, Constance M. *American Humor; A Study of the National Character*. New York: Harcourt, Brace & Co., 1931.

Sloane, William. *Children's Books in England and America in the Seventeenth Century: A History and a Checklist*. New York: King's Crown Press, Columbia University, 1955.

Smith, Henry Nash. *Virgin Land: The American West as Symbol and Myth*. Cambridge, Mass.: Harvard University Press, 1950.

Smith, Timothy. *Revivalism and Social Reform*. New York: Abingdon Press, [1957].

Somkin, Fred. *Unquiet Eagle: Memory and Desire in the Idea of American Freedom, 1815-1860*. Ithaca, N.Y.: Cornell University Press, 1967.

Stern, Bernhard J. *The Family, Past and Present*. New York: Appleton-Century, 1938.

Taylor, William R. *Cavalier and Yankee*. New York: George Braziller, 1961.

Tyler, Alice F. *Freedom's Ferment*. Minneapolis: University of Minnesota Press, 1944.

Van Nostrand, Albert. *The Denatured Novel*. New York: Bobbs-Merrill, 1956.

Welsh, Mary M. *Catherine Maria Sedgwick*. Washington, D.C.: Catholic University Press, 1937.

White, Leonard. *The Jacksonians: A Study in Administrative History, 1829-1861*. New York: Macmillan Co., 1954.

Wishey, Bernard. *The Child and the Republic*. Philadelphia: University of Pennsylvania Press, 1968.

Wohl, R. Richard. "The 'Rags to Riches Story': An Episode of Secular Idealism." In *Class, Status and Power*, edited by Reinhart Bendix and Seymour M. Lipset. Glencoe, Ill.: The Free Press, 1953.

Zuckerman, Michael. "The Nursery Tales of Horatio Alger." *American Quarterly* 24 (May 1972):191-209.

Index

Abbott, Jacob, 14, 32-33, 44, 48, 49, 50, 63, 77, 78, 81, 90, 97, 151, 164n.45; *Caleb in the Country* 81; *Franconia Tales* 44, 63; *Rollo At School* 50, 76; *The Rollo Philosophy* 77

Abolition; *see* anti-slavery sentiment

Adams, Henry, 119

Adams, William Taylor, 119, 121, 123, 128, 129, 132; 'Great Western' Series; 'Lake Shore' Series; 'Yacht Club' Series 119; *Poor and Proud* 119-123, 127-128, 129,130,132, 133, 134, 140-141

Adelaide, 63

Alden, Joseph; *An Old Revolutionary Soldier* 88, 106-107

Alfred Raymond; or, A Mother's Influence, 123

Alger, Horatio, 12, 121, 173n.4, 174n.28

All The Happy Endings (Papashivly), 12, 173n.24

The American Adam (Lewis), 11

American Colonization Society, 114

American Reform Tract and Book Society, 111, 172n.76

American Sunday School Union (ASSU), 21-23, 153, 172n.76

Anti-Intellectualism in America (Hofstadter), 163n.23)

Anti-slavery sentiment, 35-36, 104, 105, 143, 171n.38, 172n.72, 172n.73; in juvenille fiction 111-116

Anti-war sentiment, 143, 171n.38;

in juvenile fiction 104-108, 117

An Appeal in Favor of That Class of Americans Called Africans (Child), 36, 115, 172n.72

Arthur, T. S.; *The Beggars*, 126

"Aunt Friendly"; *Bound Out* 47,48

"Aunt Julia", 103, 109, 110; *The Temperance Boys* 103-104; *The Brandy Drops* 109-110

Authorship of juvenile fiction, 20-21, 31-40; Southern, 32, 163n.34; after 1850, 118-141, 156-158

Avery, Gillian; *Nineteenth Century Children* 165n.25

Baker, Mrs. Harriet, 129

Barbauld, Anna L., 20, 34

Beecher, Catherine, 25, 26, 29; *The Duty of American Women to Their Children* 26; *Treatise on Domestic Economy* 25

Beale, Mrs. O. A. S., 130, 132, 133; *Georgy Lee* 130, 133; "Shadow in the House" 130-132, 133

Belle and Lily, 129

Blacks; *see* Negroes

Blind Susan, 61

The Bobbin Bay (Thayer), 170n.9, 174n.28

Book of Fables (Goodrich), 66

Bound Out ("Aunt Friendly"), 47, 48

Boy Life on the Prairie (Garland), 46

Bradley, M. E., *Douglass Farm* 73

The Brandy Drops ("Aunt Julia"), 109-110

Branch, E. Douglas, 155
Brown, Herbert Ross, 155
Bruce, Carlton, 84, 85, 88; "Story of Tom Restless" 84-85
Bushnell, Horace; *Christian Nurture* 90, 157, 158, 163n.28, 169 n.68

Cabot, Eliza Lee; *see* Eliza Follen
Caleb in the Country, (Abbott, Jacob) 81
Cavalier and Yankee, (Taylor) 11, 163n.33
Calhoun, Arthur; *A Social History of the American Family* 173n.23
Cardell, William 24, 27, 47, 48, 118, 159, 162n.3; *The Happy Family* 24; *Story of Jack Halyard* 20, 48, 159
Cawelti, John, 12
Channing, William Ellery, 37
Charity, 60, 67, 98-102, 147; changing views of 124-127, 138, 166 n.51, 173n.12
Charles Ashton, The Boy That Would be a Soldier, 105-106, 107
Cheap Repository Tracts, (More) 38
"Cheerful Cherry" (Goodrich) 86
Chesboro, Mrs., *Smiles and Tears* 61
The Child and the Republic (Wishey), 13, 28
The Child's Friend, 32
Child, Lydia Maria, 15, 33-37, 39, 42, 73, 81, 111-112, 113-115, 148; *An Appeal in Favor of That Class of Americans Called Africans* 36, 115, 172n.72; *Evenings in New England* 20, 34, 113, 162n.5; *The Frugal Housewife* 36; *Hobomok* 34; *The Little Girl's Own Book* 102, *The*

Mother's Book 35
Child nurture, 9, 13, 19, 68, 138; authors attitudes to, 33, 151-155; responsibility for, 28-29; social function of. 145-151
The Child of Want and Misery, 59
Childhood, or, Little Alice, 74
Children, Training, *see* Child Nurture
Children's fiction; *see* Juvenile fiction
Christian Nurture (Bushnell), 90, 157, 163n.28, 169n.68
Cities, 26; authors attitudes to, 44-45, 122-124
Class consciousness, 98-102, 110, 116-117, 136, 143, 165n.25, 170 n.30
Clemens, Samuel L., *Tom Sawyer* 10
The Contrast, 56-57
Conquest and Self-Conquest, 65
The Cooper's Son, 134
The Country Schoolhouse, 74
The Crusade Against Slavery (Filler), 172n.72, 172n.76

The Daisy, 82
Death, portrayal of in juvenile fiction, 10, 41, 55, 60-65, 67, 137
Demos, John; *A Little Commonwealth*, 166n.41, 168n.41
Dick and His Friend Fidus, 87-88
The Discovery of Asylum (Rothman), 59, 168n.36, 173n.13
Dodgson, Charles L., 161n.4
Douglass Farm (Bradley), 73
The Duty of American Women to Their Children (Beecher, 26

Edgarton, Miss, "The Mysterious Benefactor", 100
Edgeworth, Maria, 20, 34, 49
Ellen Leslie (McIntosh), 153

192

Sunday School Libraries, 22, 112
Sunday School Movement, 21-23,
  55; *see also* American Sunday
  School Union

Taylor, William; *Cavalier and
  Yankee*, 11, 163n.33
Thayer, William; *The Bobbin Boy*,
  170n.9, 174n.28
Temperance, 46, 52, 66, 104, 108-
  111, 117, 143
The Temperance Boys ("Aunt
  Julia"), 103-104
Tocqueville, Alexis de, 14, 79, 145,
  146, 150, 175n.17
Tom Sawyer (Clemens), 10
Treatise on Domestic Economy
  (Beecher), 25
Trollope, Anthony, 23
Turner, Nat, 111
Tuthill, Louisa, 33; *Get Money*
  129, 130, 135
Twilight Tales (Follen), 112

Venable, William T., 15
Virgin Land (Smith), 11

Walter Browning, 116
Washington, George, 49, 71, 74,
  98, 106, 107
The Way To Do Good, 101
Webster, Daniel, 29, 163n.30; "In-
  fluence of Women" 163n.30
Wishey, Bernard, 13; *The Child
  and the Republic* 13, 28
"Well Enough for the Vulgar", 110
The Well-Spent Hour (Follen),
  112
Whittier, John Greenleaf, 37
Willis, Nathaniel (Editor), *Youth's
  Companion* 19

Youth's Companion, 19, 82, 111,
  116

Zuckerman, Michael; "The Nursery Tales of Horatio Alger",
  174n.28